5000-1

THE LEICESTER CITY STORY

5000-1

THE LEICESTER CITY STORY

HOW WE BEAT THE ODDS TO BECOME PREMIER LEAGUE CHAMPIONS

ROB TANNER

ICON

Published in the UK in 2016
by Icon Books Ltd, Omnibus Business Centre,
39–41 North Road, London N7 9DP
email: info@iconbooks.com
www.iconbooks.com

Sold in the UK, Europe and Asia
by Faber & Faber Ltd, Bloomsbury House,
74–77 Great Russell Street,
London WC1B 3DA or their agents

Distributed in the UK, Europe and Asia
by Grantham Book Services,
Trent Road, Grantham NG31 7XQ

Distributed in the USA
by Publishers Group West,
1700 Fourth Street, Berkeley, CA 94710

Distributed in Australia and New Zealand
by Allen & Unwin Pty Ltd,
PO Box 8500, 83 Alexander Street,
Crows Nest, NSW 2065

Distributed in South Africa
by Jonathan Ball, Office B4, The District,
41 Sir Lowry Road, Woodstock 7925

Distributed in India by Penguin Books India,
7th Floor, Infinity Tower – C, DLF Cyber City,
Gurgaon 122002, Haryana

Distributed in Canada by Publishers Group Canada,
76 Stafford Street, Unit 300
Toronto, Ontario M6J 2S1

ISBN: 978-178578-151-3

Typeset in New Baskerville by Marie Doherty

Printed and bound in the UK by Clays Ltd, St Ives plc

ABOUT THE AUTHOR

Rob Tanner is the *Leicester Mercury*'s chief football writer. He has been the newspaper's Leicester City correspondent for the past seven seasons, reporting on the club's rise from the doldrums of League One to the Premier League title. He lives in Tamworth, Staffordshire, with his wife Jayne and his dog Molly.

Alan Smith is a former Leicester City and Arsenal striker who, alongside Gary Lineker, helped fire the Foxes to the Second Division title in 1984/85. He is a co-commentator and studio pundit for Sky Sports, has been the voice of EA Sports' FIFA video game series since 2011, and writes regularly for the *Daily Telegraph*.

To my late mother, Madeline.
I hope I have made you proud.

CONTENTS

LIST OF PHOTOGRAPHS

Claudio Ranieri celebrates victory away at Sunderland,
10 April 2016

Wes Morgan heads Leicester level at Old Trafford,
1 May 2016

The Man Utd match ends 1-1 and all eyes turn towards
Tottenham, 1 May 2016

Leicester City are crowned Premier League champions,
7 May 2016

Wes Morgan becomes a Premier League champion for the
first time, 7 May 2016

Andy King, Danny Drinkwater and Matty James celebrate,
7 May 2016

Claudio Ranieri celebrates with Kasper Schmeichel,
7 May 2016

ACKNOWLEDGEMENTS

Thanks to my wife Jayne; my family and friends for their love and support; my colleagues and journalistic peers for their encouragement and advice; and to the *Leicester Mercury* for giving me the opportunity to cover this remarkable story for the newspaper.

Above all, thanks to Leicester City for giving me the most unforgettable season of my career.

FOREWORD

by Alan Smith

So much has changed at Leicester City since I first walked through those dressing-room doors. For a start, Filbert Street has been flattened, replaced by a block of flats. A few hundred yards up the road, the King Power Stadium speaks eloquently of the club's progress.

As part of that, no longer do the players get changed for training at the ground before jumping in cars to drive across town. In my time, Belvoir Drive did not boast much in the way of facilities.

Mind you, neither did the team ever really cause a stir. Sure, we won promotion in 1983 before enjoying some good times in the top flight. But nothing like this. Nothing nearly so momentous. I think the closest we came to upsetting the odds was beating Manchester United 3-0 one memorable afternoon.

For me personally, then, it has been an absolute thrill to witness Leicester's heroics first-hand, to commentate for

Sky on several matches in a season that will clearly find a major place in football folklore.

Chatting to the fans before and after games, they couldn't quite believe what was going on. A stunned, disbelieving look clouded their features as they looked to me for some kind of reassurance.

Not that I knew. I mean, this was new territory for everyone – when a club outside the established Premier League elite not only gatecrashed the party but completely stole the show.

Make no mistake, these lads have cemented their place in sporting history. Fifty years from now, people will be able to reel off the regular starting XI, from Kasper Schmeichel all the way through to Jamie Vardy.

Supporters will reminisce about key games when somebody stepped forward to make the difference. Vardy's brilliant goals, the match-winning skills of Riyad Mahrez, the incredible energy of N'Golo Kanté or the inspirational fortitude of captain Wes Morgan: whatever the tale, it will pass into legend.

In the immediate aftermath of victory, you can't really grasp it. Emotions are running too high, the blood pumping too fast. But as the months and years pass, the players concerned will gradually come to appreciate where this achievement stands in the firmament.

The answer is high, perhaps at the very top, and for that we can all join in the celebrations. The Foxes have confirmed that romance isn't dead, that the impossible dream can still be realised, just when we thought that money ruled.

Leicester City: Premier League champions. Run that one by me again?

Alan Smith
May 2016

AUTHOR'S NOTE

In 2009 I joined the *Leicester Mercury* as the newspaper's chief football writer, covering Leicester City Football Club. In the years that followed I have witnessed the club's rise from League One to the Premier League summit. In 2014/15, as the club battled to avoid a return to the Championship, I started to write a blog for the *Leicester Mercury* website, covering the team's fortunes, the goings-on at the club and the feeling throughout the city. I continued to do so long after Nigel Pearson's men pulled off their sensational survival bid in May 2015.

As the 2015/16 season rumbled on, with the momentum carried forward from the previous campaign showing no sign of slowing, it became clear that this story was one that warranted telling in full, so I began to write a book – this book. There have been so many moments over the past twelve months that have defied belief; moments that, looking back, seem almost unreal. In an effort to capture each twist and turn in this incredible season, I have included blog-posts from throughout the season to provide snapshots of the key moments, telling the story as it happened and trying to convince myself that it really did.

INTRODUCTION

Sunday 15 May 2016. Stamford Bridge, London. Leicester City's final game of the season has been over for some time. The ground is empty and the only sound is the occasional smack of a seat springing back to the closed position as Chelsea staff patrol the stands, picking up litter.

The press bench is empty. The other journalists are either inside, feverishly trying to meet their deadlines, or have already left to catch the trains at Fulham Broadway station. I am, pretty much, alone on the press bench. I have just pressed 'send' on my final report of the season. I puff out my cheeks, look around the ground and reflect on what an incredible, almost unbelievable, season it has been.

It is my first chance to take in what I have witnessed over the previous year. I have followed the Foxes every single step of the way, from the incredible fight for Premier League survival the previous season to their astonishing transformation into title challengers and, ultimately, champions of England. It has been a whirlwind.

From the euphoria of City winning seven of their final nine games of 2014/15 to claw back a seven-point deficit to safety and remain in the Premier League, to the disappointment and shock when manager Nigel Pearson was sacked after his relationship with the club's owners soured, I was there.

From the mixed reaction to the appointment of Claudio Ranieri and the sadness at the departure of star player Esteban Cambiasso, to City's surprising but delightful start to the season, I was watching, recording every kick and every comment for the *Leicester Mercury*.

Then, as the season progressed and City edged closer and closer to achieving history, something nearly everyone would have said was completely impossible, I looked on from the press benches of the biggest grounds in England in astonishment, but also delight. Even now, at Stamford Bridge, the home of the dethroned title-holders, who have just warmly welcomed City, the new champions of England, it is hard to comprehend exactly what I have witnessed. How was this possible?

You could have had odds of 5000-1 from bookmakers on City winning a first-ever title, the same odds as finding Elvis Presley alive. The probability of them becoming champions was 0.02 per cent, using the bookmakers' calculations. There was just no way this was supposed to happen.

Ranieri was an experienced manager having taken charge at some of the biggest clubs in Europe in his time, but he had never won a domestic title before and had previously been sacked after a disastrous spell in charge of the Greek national team. They even lost to the Faroe Islands. His City squad was mainly made up of players who had been rejected and cast aside by other clubs, and players others didn't want or didn't rate. They were branded the 'Misfits'.

Leicester City hadn't exactly had a trophy-laden history either. In its 132-year existence, the club had never won the league title or the FA Cup. There had been moments of success. City had won three League Cups and reached four FA Cup finals, and there had been some special moments, mainly promotion play-off final wins at Wembley.

Teams like Leicester City are not supposed to challenge the established elite of the Premier League. Manchester United, Manchester City, Arsenal and Chelsea have dominated the title almost completely in the modern era. Only one other team, Blackburn Rovers, had won the title since the Premier League was formed in 1992.

I have to confess, even as the incredible events of the season were unfolding before my eyes, with City winning week after week, I didn't think they could win the title. Football is in my blood. It is all I ever wanted to do, play and watch football, but I had become programmed to believe that there was no romance in the game anymore. I was wrong. It wasn't until the Foxes won at Manchester City in February that I felt this could be possible, that Leicester could challenge for the title.

It is only now, as I look around Stamford Bridge, that I can start to comprehend what has happened. Leicester City have won the Premier League by a huge margin of ten points. They have smashed it. The favourites for relegation before a ball was kicked in August have produced the greatest sporting shock in history.

This has to be the most amazing sporting underdog story of all time. The Premier League will never be the same again.

SUMMER 2015

A SUMMER OF DISCONTENT

At the end of March 2015, Leicester City were seven points adrift of safety and rooted to the foot of the Premier League table, a position they had been in for the previous four months. Nigel Pearson's side had been written off as relegation certainties. Even Pearson himself was thinking, with nine games left, that the task was just too great, but after one of the most dramatic transformations in English football history, City survived, and with a game to spare.

There were several factors contributing to their recovery, among them the growing influence of loan signing Robert Huth and Pearson's switch to a three centre-back, wing-back system. The arrival into the team of Marc Albrighton, who had previously been out in the cold for longer than Scott of the Antarctic, had provided some much-needed energy, while Jamie Vardy had been given a run in the team and was starting to display some of the form that would light up the Premier League in 2015/16.

And at the heart of the team was Esteban Cambiasso, City's talismanic midfielder, the most decorated player in Argentinian football history and the subject of every City fan's devotion. Not since Roberto Mancini had the Foxes had such an illustrious, internationally renowned player within their skulk. City fans had spent most of the season in disbelief that a player of Cambiasso's pedigree had chosen to join City's desperate fight for survival and any concerns that he had done so simply for one last payday had been dismissed by a succession of superb performances.

It was Cambiasso who had set the ball rolling in City's Great Escape, scoring the first goal in the 2-1 win over West Ham United at the King Power Stadium on 4 April 2015, with late substitute and club stalwart Andy King scoring a dramatic winner. A week later Vardy had scored a last-minute winner at West Bromwich Albion and City were starting to gain belief and momentum. Then it was three wins on the bounce as King again scored late on as Swansea City were dispatched on home soil, before Vardy was again the match-winner in a crucial victory away at relegation rivals Burnley, a defeat from which the Clarets would not recover.

There was the home defeat to eventual champions Chelsea but any concerns that that would trigger another collapse were quickly dispelled as Newcastle United and then Southampton were dispatched in style, setting up a crucial away clash with Sunderland, another side who were mounting a less dramatic but equally effective battle to beat the drop, at the Stadium of Light.

The game was instantly forgettable, but the result, a 0-0 stalemate, was enough to ensure City remained among the elite of Premier League football for another season at least and the scenes at the final whistle would live long in the memory of the City fans who had only dared to dream that what they had witnessed was possible.

Pearson was the toast of English football for masterminding such an extraordinary achievement; although that certainly hadn't been the case with members of the media during what had been a troubled second half of the campaign, punctuated by touchline spats with first a supporter and then the Crystal Palace midfielder James McArthur. There followed a phantom sacking of Pearson by the club's owners and further spats with journalists, most notably his branding of Ian Baker, of Wardles news agency, an 'ostrich' when the journalist queried Pearson's claim that the team had its critics.

Pearson is a complex man. Brusque, authoritative and intimidating at times, his public persona was that of a sergeant major figure who didn't suffer fools gladly and was quick to temper when faced with what he perceived as poorly chosen questions. He could be all that at times. However, over the four-and-a-half seasons I covered Leicester City under his management, I also saw the other side to him, the side that existed away from the microscope of managing a club of City's size and with the weight of expectation placed upon it.

When I first started covering City, he could be incredibly difficult to deal with. He could stop a press conference with one curt answer. I had to learn, and sometimes I learned the hard way, how to approach him. For instance, he seemed to have a deep-seated mistrust of the media in general and was always on his guard for the question he believed had a hidden agenda. You didn't try to put words into Pearson's mouth or offer leading questions. That was pure folly. If a question started: 'Nigel, would you say …' then I knew there would be an instant rebuff: 'Those are your words, your view,' he would instantly fire back. I learned to keep my questions short, sharp and straight to the point. Don't beat about the bush. If there was a question that had to be asked, however unpalatable, and Pearson knew it was coming then you had to just ask it. He would lose respect for you as a journalist if you didn't.

Over time, I could predict how he would approach post-match press conferences. If City had won, he would be downbeat, matter-of-fact in his responses to questions. He often came across as gruff. But when City had lost or were going through a difficult time, he would turn on the charm, and he did have a fair bit of it to turn on. He never seemed completely at ease with the media; it seemed to be an irritant he could have well done without, although he once shocked me during City's Great Escape season when he declared he was enjoying talking to the media. By then it was no longer just me and BBC Radio Leicester's Ian Stringer sat around a table down the training ground. The media spotlight of the Premier League was now shining on the media suite at the King Power Stadium, which had now been refitted for the nation's press pack. Pearson's pre-match press conferences would last up to 50 minutes and he would give detailed answers lasting several minutes to each question. However, he was reluctant to give the journalists the sound bites they craved

Many thought that Pearson either didn't know how to work the media or just simply didn't want to play the media's game. The latter was more accurate.

One way he did use the media was to create a siege mentality within his squad by fostering the feeling that the media was after them. He got the best out of his players when there was a bubble created around them and the training ground, sheltering them from any perceived negativity either within the media or from the outside world.

Towards the end of his final season, he mentioned negativity towards his players from within the media on more than one occasion, which baffled many of the regulars at his press conferences because they had been regularly praising his players for their performances. Many writers and broadcasters, including myself, were repeatedly pointing out that Pearson's side weren't far away from being a team that could pick up results in the Premier League. They had been in every game but were repeatedly being punished for momentary lapses defensively. They were obviously giving their all and fighting for their manager and the club, but were discovering how cruel the Premier League could be at times.

I never questioned him about this media negativity to which he referred, but Ian Baker did, resulting in the now famous 'ostrich' rant. Pearson knew he was out of order and apologised to Baker the next day; but such incidents, and the resulting media coverage, were never going to go down well with the City ownership. Likewise when three young City players, including Pearson's own son, were sacked for off-pitch misdemeanours on an end-of-season tour of Thailand. The owners are fiercely proud of their heritage and their reputation is crucially important to them, especially as they have close associations with the King of Thailand. Their connection with City and ownership of a club in the Premier League, the most watched and popular league in Thailand, had boosted their public status, but this was a bitter blow to their own credibility and image. Action was inevitable, although no one expected it to lead to the departure of Pearson.

The last time I spoke to Pearson as City manager was just before the club's end-of-season awards dinner. I met him in his office at the stadium, a large room, minimally decorated with large black sofas arranged in squares, giving it more than a passing resemblance to a high-end airport waiting lounge. There was the sense that Pearson didn't spend a particularly large amount of time in this room. This was where he would entertain opposition managers and coaching staff after matches and on this occasion it was the venue for my last interview with Pearson before the team flew to Thailand.

He spoke of his optimism for the future, the development of his plans and the solid foundations now in place, upon which the club could build. He also spoke of his own public image, his reluctance to be a celebrity and how he would choose to do things differently in certain situations in future; but, fundamentally, he insisted he would not change.

He was true to his word.

Pearson's sacking came on 30 June and the news came like a bolt from the blue. It had been two weeks since the sacking of the three young professionals and City were set to return to pre-season training the following week. The first inkling of what was to follow late on that Tuesday evening came when the bookmakers slashed the odds on Pearson being sacked, a sure sign that something was happening. Either someone who had an idea about what was taking place had placed a huge bet on Pearson being sacked, trying to make a killing before the news broke, or someone had leaked the information. The bookmakers were to play a major role in the remarkable twists and turns of the search for Pearson's successor over the next few weeks. Nevertheless, the change in the odds sparked a frenzy among the media and it wasn't long before the club confirmed that Pearson had been sacked.

There weren't many City fans who thought it was good news, although there was always a small section of supporters who weren't Pearson fans because of the way he came across publicly from time to time. The players were due to return to full training and City had already begun their preparations for the new season. Pearson had even made his first signing of the summer, Austria captain Christian Fuchs, who had said it was after a conversation with Pearson that he was convinced to come to the King Power Stadium after leaving Schalke on a free transfer. Pearson had also spent £3 million on the permanent signing of Huth, a deal that City fans had seen as absolutely vital, and £7 million on Japan striker Shinji Okazaki, a long-term target brought in from Bundesliga side Mainz. The early business had stoked the sense of optimism among supporters, but now there was uncertainty: in which direction would City turn now? There was a fear, not just among City supporters, that the foundations which had been laid over the previous three-and-a-half seasons would be ripped up and the progress City had made under Pearson would stall.

City fans had seen it before when Pearson was allowed to leave for Hull City in 2010. Paulo Sousa, twice a European Cup winner as a player, had come in for a disastrous nine-game spell in charge before former England manager Sven-Göran Eriksson arrived. After spending millions on over a dozen new signings, he was sacked just 13 games into the 2011/12 season. Now there were fears of another boom and bust scenario.

LEICESTER MERCURY BLOG, 8 JULY 2015
LIFE AFTER PEARSON

In the statement released following the shock sacking of Nigel Pearson, the owners of Leicester City appealed to the fans to trust them.

'We trust that the club's supporters will recognise that the owners have always acted with the best interests of the club at heart and with the club's long-term future as their greatest priority,' it read.

Trust has to be earned and over the past five years the efforts of the owners in securing the club's financial position and laying the foundations for the push to the Premier League deserve that trust.

Like their cash, the owners have plenty in the bank when it comes to trust from City fans.

Actions speak louder than words, which is a good job as they have very rarely spoken publicly in that time.

But that trust is not blind faith and City fans will be waiting, like everyone else, to see who will be Pearson's replacement and whether their judgement over the change of manager has been sound or flawed.

Since sacking Pearson there has been no word from City, not one syllable, about how the hunt for the next boss is going. City have closed ranks, shut up shop and decided to try to identify the next manager in clandestine fashion.

The silence creates uncertainty in the minds of supporters. It creates doubt.

Did they have a plan in place before they sacked Pearson? Did they have an idea of which direction they were about to go in? Will they get the right man in to build on the solid foundations now in place? Are they starting completely from scratch? How long will this process take?

I know fans are asking these questions because they have asked me them on social media. I cannot answer, other than to say I hope they have it all in hand because the longer the process drags on the more disruptive it will be to City's pre-season.

City have not finished their summer squad strengthening and it is clear from the ongoing attempts to sign N'Golo Kanté and the £12 million offer for Charlie Austin that City are pressing ahead without a manager.

The problem is players are reluctant to jump to sign for a club when there is such mystery surrounding the identity of the next manager. Who would pick City over an alternative club when there is uncertainty over whether the man coming in would actually want them?

The players currently at the club are professional and resilient. This will not be the first time they have experienced a change in leadership.

Craig Shakespeare and Steve Walsh are likewise stoic figures and will be giving their all on the training ground to prepare the players despite the doubt that must be in their own minds about their own futures.

But the new manager will need time in pre-season to make his own arrangements and set up City how he wants them to play and the longer the current situation drags on the less time City will have to prepare thoroughly.

The uncertainty and instability will impact on City's start to the season.

City appear to be no nearer to making an appointment. If reports are true, Guus Hiddink is going to take some convincing, while it is believed there has been no approach to Bolton for bookmakers' favourite Neil Lennon.

In fact, there doesn't seem to be any hint of an outstanding candidate, which raises the question how far down the line City actually are in identifying the new manager.

I refuse to believe that they didn't have a plan when Pearson was sacked. Billionaire businessmen don't become successful by not thinking several moves ahead when they make a big decision.

But only time will tell.

In the meantime, City fans just have to keep the faith.

City were playing their cards very close to their chest in their search for the next manager and that had created a void for supporters who were so hungry for any scrap of information that they, and the bookmakers, would feed on any nonsense. The names linked with the Leicester vacancy ranged from Martin O'Neill to Jürgen Klopp, and at one point the bookies stopped taking bets on Sacramento Republic's manager Predrag Radosavljević.

Eventually, after two weeks of intrigue and high farce, City's search for their next manager came full circle with the appointment of Claudio Ranieri. The vastly experienced manager had been quoted by Italian media as saying he would be interested in talking to City about the position right at the start of the process but had never been considered a huge favourite for the job, despite his impressive CV.

However, in terms of what the owners wanted, Ranieri ticked the boxes. He had a proven record at club level, although his previous appointment as head coach of the Greek national team had been a disaster. He had managed some of the biggest clubs in Europe and some of the games' most high-profile players, and he had enjoyed success. His reputation around the world would raise the club's profile once again and repair some of the damage done by the events of the summer.

He was the perfect fit for the owners, but the City fans and the media would need a lot more convincing.

LEICESTER MERCURY BLOG, 13 JULY 2015
RANIERI APPOINTED

Claudio Ranieri is the new manager of Leicester City.

City announced this afternoon on Twitter that the 63-year-old Italian is Nigel Pearson's successor at the King Power Stadium.

Ranieri has signed a three-year contract to lead City into their second season in the Premier League and has met his new squad at their training camp in Austria.

'I'm so glad to be here in a club with such a great tradition as Leicester City,' said Ranieri.

'I have worked at many great clubs, in many top leagues, but since I left Chelsea I have dreamt of another chance to work in the best league in the world again.

'I wish to thank the owner, his son and all the executives of the club for the opportunity they are giving me.

'Now I've only one way for returning their trust: squeeze all my energies into getting the best results for the team.'

Club vice-chairman Aiyawatt Srivaddhanaprabha said it was Ranieri's impressive CV, having managed some of the biggest clubs in Europe, including Inter Milan, Roma, Juventus, Chelsea and Monaco, which made them decide he was the right man for the job.

'It is my great pleasure to welcome Claudio Ranieri – a man of remarkable experience and knowledge that will lead us into the next phase of our long-term plan for Leicester City,' said Aiyawatt.

'His achievements in the game, his knowledge of English football and his record of successfully coaching some of the world's finest players made him the outstanding candidate for the job and his ambitions for the future reflect our own.

'To have attracted one of the world's elite managers speaks volumes both for the progress Leicester City has made in recent years and for the potential that remains for the Club's long-term development.'

Ranieri publicly threw his hat into the ring over a week ago following the sacking of Pearson and said the prospect of managing in the Premier League was very attractive to him.

His appointment brings to an end a two-week search for City's next manager with former Holland boss Guus Hiddink and former City manager Martin O'Neill sounded out for the position, but both declined.

Pearson's former assistants Craig Shakespeare and Steve Walsh are currently overseeing the training camp in Bad Radkersburg but it is not yet known whether they will stay on under Ranieri.

⚽

THE TINKERMAN

To say that the appointment of Claudio Ranieri received a mixed reaction is an understatement. While the club's vice-chairman, Aiyawatt Srivaddhanaprabha, said in a statement announcing Ranieri's appointment that City had attracted 'one of the world's elite managers', there were many who didn't share his lofty appraisal of Ranieri's credentials.

The Italian had been sacked the previous November after a disastrous spell as manager of the Greek national team. He had lasted just four games and suffered the ignominy of a home defeat to the Faroe Islands. One game later – another defeat – his two-year contract had been torn up.

'Claudio Ranieri? Really?' tweeted City legend Gary Lineker, who went on to add: 'Claudio Ranieri is clearly experienced, but this is an uninspired choice by Leicester.'

Lineker's was not a lone voice on social media. Another former City striker, Tony Cottee said he was 'astonished' by the appointment while former Tottenham Hotspur manager Harry Redknapp also tweeted his surprise that Ranieri was back in the Premier League: 'Ranieri is a nice guy, but he's done well to get the Leicester job. After what happened with Greece, I'm surprised he can walk back into the Premier League.'

While some posts on fans' forums and social media seemed happy to have Ranieri as Pearson's successor, the majority were extremely sceptical. The reign of Eriksson was still fresh in their memory: a period of huge upheaval as millions were spent on dozens of players without the team ever looking like it would become a cohesive unit. Pearson had come in and sorted all of that out, slowly and sensibly building a team that had fulfilled the City fans' dreams. While many had been irritated by the public spats, they had been willing to accept the negative headlines they caused because they knew that deep down Pearson was a good manager who was able to foster a fantastic team spirit among his troops, and he had a great backroom team too.

It had been 11 years since Ranieri had left Chelsea and despite an impressive looking CV, packed with the names of some of the biggest clubs in Europe, Ranieri had never stayed anywhere longer than two seasons since leaving Stamford Bridge. It felt like, at best, this was a short-term appointment, and at worst a disaster waiting to happen.

When the Srivaddhanaprabha family and their King Power empire had taken over the club in August, 2010, there was a nervousness among the City fans, who didn't have to look too far to see how overseas ownerships could turn sour. Portsmouth nearly went out of business completely under the ownership of several different foreign investors, while just down the M6, Birmingham City's owner Carson Yeung was jailed for money laundering and the club was edging towards its own financial crisis. Over in Cardiff, Malaysian Vincent Tan had enraged supporters by changing the club's traditional colours of blue to red, which was deemed to be a lucky colour in Malaysia.

There were initially fears the Thais would do something similar when they bought the club from Milan Mandarić, that the price to be paid for their huge cash injection into the club would be City's soul, its heritage, its heart. Those fears were short-lived as not only did the Srivaddhanaprabha family cherish the traditions of the club, they promoted the club's heritage and fostered its close links with the Leicester community, while still striving to create a club that was ready for the globalisation of the Premier League.

They did introduce elements of their own culture to the club, which are still evident today. The Thai flag flies proudly around the King Power Stadium; blue flags adorned with Buddhist prayers for good fortune are hung like bunting around the stadium and around the tunnel area; and groups of Buddhist monks are regular visitors, at the invitation of the owners. Decked in their traditional orange and tan robes, the monks were brought in to bless Pearson and his team, the home dressing room and even the goalposts. They are reverent figures, but there is also a comical aspect about them as they often cling to Leicester City merchandise bags and have more than a touch of the wide-eyed tourist about them as they are herded through the bowels of the King Power Stadium.

The irony may be lost on them that while they are a long way from their own temple, they are visiting an equally holy place to City fans. This is the place where the folk of Leicester come every Saturday to worship, to sing songs and even say a few prayers to ask for divine intervention. The common link between an English football experience and a religious one is strong so the monks are not completely out of place, although the first time they were seen at the stadium was a surreal moment.

They have become regular visitors now to such an extent that it is no longer a novelty for the players, who have become accustomed to having water thrown at them as they are blessed while getting ready for a game.

But it is through their financial might that the owners have really made their mark at the club. Writing off £103 million of loans into equity demonstrated their commitment to the cause and the owners have become extremely popular with the City fans. However, after Pearson's departure and the appointment of Ranieri on a three-year contract, some sections of the supporters were starting to question whether the owners really knew what they were doing.

On the face of it, Ranieri was a complete departure from Pearson. Pearson was a players' manager, a man's man, a working-class hero who played by his own rules and refused to compromise his views for the media or any employer. He was authoritative, a natural leader.

In contrast, Ranieri is a genial, well-mannered and good natured man, but his inability to master English when he first took over at Chelsea hampered his ability to make a positive first impression on the English football public and his clumsy phrasing of English while at Stamford Bridge contributed to him being seen as something of a comic figure. The fact that Eriksson and then José Mourinho were so publicly courted as replacements by new Chelsea owner Roman Abramovich, who took over Chelsea in 2003 and immediately looked for a new manager, didn't help Ranieri, who was seen as a dead man walking, although there was plenty of admiration for him as well because of the dignity he showed throughout that situation.

Closer inspection of his career provided more heart that Ranieri could be the man to take the club to the next level. Early in his coaching career he had forged a reputation for taking smaller clubs and building them up so they could challenge the elite. He had taken Cagliari from Serie C to Serie A. He would confess this had been the most rewarding moment of his career to date. After a two-year spell in charge of Napoli, where he gave Gianfranco Zola his debut, he took Fiorentina up to Serie A and won the Coppa Italia and Supercoppa Italiana. At Valencia he put the foundations in place for their future success in the Champions League – but then spent a season at Atlético Madrid, who were relegated amidst mounting financial crisis.

During his time at Stamford Bridge he transformed the team, bringing in youthful players such as Frank Lampard and Joe Cole, while nurturing emerging talent like John Terry, Robert Huth (who would be such a stalwart of his City team) and Carlton Cole, and he led them to a Champions League semi-final and second in the Premier League before he was sacked. The foundations he laid in place would provide the platform for the success Chelsea enjoyed under Mourinho.

After Chelsea he returned to Valencia before heading back to Italy for spells in charge of Parma, Juventus, Roma and Inter Milan, with varying degrees of success, although he was unable to land a league title, before he headed to AS Monaco, taking them back up to the top flight of French football and leading them to runners-up in Ligue 1. As managerial records go, there are not many coaches in the European game who can produce such an impressive CV.

Above all, though, he was renowned as the 'Tinkerman' for his constant changing of his Chelsea team.

The concept of squad rotation was alien to English football at the turn of the century. A manager was expected to pick his best team week after week. Only injury or a loss of form would alter how a team would line up. In contrast, Ranieri would make changes on a regular basis; and he was heavily criticised for some of his substitutions in Chelsea's Champions League semi-final defeat to Monaco in 2004.

As he would later point out, every manager in the Premier League is now a Tinkerman, as squad rotation is now commonplace, but he was the original Tinkerman, the pioneer for all Tinkermen. As a result, many City fans feared he would rip up the team that had finished the previous season so strongly and dismantle the solid foundations that had been laid over the previous three years. There were also concerns that Ranieri would replace Pearson's assistants, Craig Shakespeare, Mike Stowell and Steve Walsh, the head of recruitment who had unearthed Riyad Mahrez.

The fears proved to be unfounded. On his appointment, Ranieri immediately flew out to City's Austrian
training camp in Bad Radkersburg to meet his new squad
and staff. The camp had been set up by Pearson and his
staff and in Pearson's absence City were going about their
pre-season preparations quietly in the scenic south-east corner of Austria. The players would cycle from their hotel to
the training facilities and back, and the evenings were spent
peacefully within the hotel compound. The remote location
made it perfect for team bonding as there were no external
distractions, although the players would confess that bore-
dom in the evenings was an issue.

City have had bad experiences of training camps in the
past, with two trips to La Manga in Spain causing national
headlines in 2000 and 2004, but there had been no such
controversy on City's trips with Pearson; even if there had
been some shenanigans, there was no one around to witness them.

Pearson's love of remote scenic places was well docu-
mented and he confirmed a rumour that he had been forced
to defend himself in the wilds of Romania while on one
solo break. While he said the Leicester folklore that he had
wrestled a bear was not true, he did have to defend himself
against a pack of wild dogs on two occasions, fighting them
off with his walking poles before diving into a patch of sting-
ing nettles to deter them a second time.

Ranieri arrived into the oasis of peace and tranquillity
to begin his reign as City boss, but while the expectation
was that he would immediately dive in and start to stamp his
authority on proceedings, Ranieri kept a watching brief for
the remainder of the trip. He left all the coaching and conditioning to Shakespeare and the staff while he looked on,
assessing each of his players and his new colleagues, flanked

by director of football Jon Rudkin and the vice-chairman who had spoken so highly of his appointment.

Ranieri met the media on his return and the charm offensive began. Ranieri's English had improved dramatically since his Chelsea days, due chiefly to the fact he had retained a home in London and visited often. But it wasn't how he spoke that surprised many in the room; rather, it was what he had to say.

'I am sure I don't want to change too many things,' he said. 'I want to change things slowly so that everyone understands me.'

Wait, was this really the Tinkerman talking about not tinkering?

It was. Ranieri said he was impressed by the talent within the squad and the organisation of the club, and he would later state that he genuinely felt the group was strong enough not to face another relegation battle. More importantly, he identified that he had to retain the services of Shakespeare, Walsh and Stowell. Not only were they a well-established team, they also presented continuity for the players from the last few seasons. The players were shaken by the shock departure of Pearson but in Shakespeare, Walsh and Stowell there was a steadying influence, a reassurance that despite Pearson's departure, the ship was still on course, just with a different captain at the helm.

It was a masterstroke from a manager who immediately demonstrated that he had no ego. This wasn't about Ranieri making his mark, this was about the evolution of a football team. It might have been understandable had he decided to cast aside all lingering reminders of Pearson's tenure and stamp his own authority on City but he knew that would be counterproductive. The coaching staff would play a huge part in Ranieri's transition.

He did bring in two of his own staff, assistant manager Paolo Benetti and fitness and conditioning coach Andrea Azzalin, but they were the only changes, except Kevin Phillips's voluntary decision to leave to join Derby County as assistant manager, to further his own coaching aspirations.

Ranieri wanted to bring in a couple of new signings before the end of the transfer window, but there was to be no dramatic overhaul of the squad. Evolution rather than revolution was his insightful strategy.

However, there was one issue that Ranieri had to address, and he had to do so immediately – the future of Esteban Cambiasso.

THE SEARCH FOR A NEW 'CHAMPION' AS CAMBIASSO DEPARTS

Leicester City fans are used to disappointment. They have experienced it on a far too frequent basis, so they are accustomed to bad news. On the pint pot half-full–half-empty scale, City fans have been almost constantly looking at the bottom of their glass. But still the news that Esteban Cambiasso had decided not to stay at the King Power Stadium was a bitter pill to swallow. Not since Roberto Mancini's fleeting stay at Filbert Street had Leicester had such an international star, a player of such quality that City fans could salivate at his every appearance.

Cambiasso is the most decorated player in Argentine history. Forget Diego Maradona and Lionel Messi, no Argentine player had ever won as much silverware and individual honours as the balding central midfielder. His career had all been about getting the job done, and while Cambiasso may not have been an eye-catching individual player like Maradona and Messi, his record was impressive. He was the cog that every wheel needed to be able to turn. He sprang to prominence in England when he was on the end of the greatest-ever team goal at a World Cup, rounding off a 26-pass move against Serbia in Germany, 2006.

His class remained long after his hair had gone.

City fans couldn't quite believe he was now pulling on a blue shirt. They worshipped him. He had his own song: 'He's magic, you know, Est-e-ban Cam-bias-so', sung to the tune of 'Magic' by Pilot. It reverberated around the King Power Stadium and every ground City visited.

A major part of his appeal was that it soon became apparent he was at City for the right reasons. He hadn't signed for a big pay cheque; he was at City because of the challenge of keeping a club like City in the Premier League. Cambiasso had never been involved in a relegation dogfight in his career before and this was a challenge he was relishing, and after winning 23 titles during his career the 34-year-old said playing in the Premier League was what he needed to do. City fans hoped it would be the final stop in his glorious journey as a player. It wasn't to be so.

Cambiasso played a huge role, both on and off the pitch, in City's remarkable escape from relegation and was crowned the club's player of the year at the end-of-season dinner. He accepted the award in the same way he played his football, with grace and humility. He bucked the trend of flash footballers. He was the only player to wear a tie at the dinner. Nothing about him personally, or professionally, was flash. He was understated and dedicated.

He had signed a one-year contract with City but long before the end of the season City were trying to get him to commit to a new deal. He said he wanted to wait until the end of the season and focus on keeping City in the Premier League before thinking about the following season.

But the end of the season came and City's talisman still hadn't made a decision. Then he left the country and was quoted by Argentine media as saying he was still undecided about his future, especially as the identity of City's new manager was uncertain, adding to the worry of the City fans. This wasn't new to City fans. The negotiations to sign him in the first place had been protracted as several people claimed to represent him, with his brother taking the lead in many of the negotiations. It had taken around five weeks of talks before Cambiasso committed to a deal.

A photo of him jogging around Leicester with teammate and fellow countryman Leo Ulloa appeared on social media and that raised hopes that he would sign again, but still there was no news. There were even suggestions he would be offered a player-manager role, but that was unfounded.

Ranieri's arrival proved to be the deciding factor. The pair had worked together at Inter Milan and it was hoped that their association would persuade Cambiasso to sign his deal. However, when Ranieri said in a press conference that he still wanted to sign Cambiasso but that he couldn't wait for ever, it seemed to force Cambiasso's hand. He didn't like being dictated to and 24 hours later, just before City's first pre-season friendly kicked off at Lincoln City, Cambiasso announced via Facebook that he had decided not to re-sign. In a statement he said he had only received City's proposal 24 hours before, around the time Ranieri appeared to make his ultimatum. However, that was just the latest of several offers from City. Negotiations had stretched back to before the final few weeks of the previous campaign.

The news overshadowed City's first run-out of the summer at Sincil Bank. Riyad Mahrez, Andrej Kramarić and Jamie Vardy were on target in a 3-1 win for Ranieri's men, but the talk afterwards wasn't about the debuts of Okazaki and Fuchs, it was about Cambiasso's announcement. How on earth were City going to fill his boots? Where were they going to find another player of such influence? After the departure of Pearson and the mixed reaction to Ranieri's appointment, this was another heavy body blow to City's preparations, and many fans feared it could be the killer blow.

After the game, on the side of the pitch at Sincil Bank, Ranieri responded to the news, thanking Cambiasso for his efforts while wearing a City shirt but declaring he would find another great 'champion' to fill the void left by Cambiasso.

His search would eventually lead to the signing of Switzerland captain Gökhan Inler for £5 million from Napoli, but it was two other players, a wide-eyed and fresh-faced youngster from France, N'Golo Kanté, and an underrated midfielder already within the City camp, Danny Drinkwater, who would ensure that Cambiasso would not be missed. That was something many City fans thought impossible.

Kanté had been on City's radar for some time. Walsh and his recruitment staff had been watching the 24-year-old for quite a while. He may have been only 5ft 6in tall, with the look of an innocent schoolboy off the pitch, but his stats showed he was incredibly competitive on it. He had been told as a youngster that he was too small to make it as a professional and while his use of the ball needed improvement, he always played with total commitment and dedication, and in his first season with SM Caen in Ligue 1 he led the stats for the top five leagues in Europe for ball recovery. In other words he would tackle his own mother if it meant regaining possession for his team.

He wasn't a complete unknown. Marseille had been trying to sign him, especially after losing Dimitri Payet to West Ham United, but it was City who managed to get the deal done – although not everyone down the training ground at

Belvoir Drive were familiar with who he was. After one of his
first training sessions with City, Kanté was standing in the car
park outside the training ground when one of the security
guards approached him. Reacting to Kanté looking a little
lost, the security guard asked him: 'Are you okay? Are you
waiting for your parents to pick you up?'

This was City's new £5.6 million signing, but when you
meet Kanté it is easy to see how the mistake is made. He has
a childlike quality as he is constantly smiling and has the
appearance of someone who is just in awe of what is happening around him. As a result, his teammates have become
very protective towards him, but he needs no protection on
the pitch, where he is as fierce a competitor as City possess.
Drinkwater has named him 'the Rash' because of his ability
to be everywhere on the pitch, and his stats this season have
shown it is an apt nickname. Walsh would later joke that
City's game plan was to play Drinkwater in the middle of
midfield and Kanté either side of him. It has felt like there
is more than one Kanté at times.

But he has shown he is much more than just a defensive
midfielder, more than just a player who can put a foot in and
win the ball. Kanté would quickly show the City fans that he
can play as well, with his surging runs from midfield a key
feature in City's counter-attacking style. His performances
would soon have the pundits, including France international
Thierry Henry, declaring him the signing of the summer.

Ironically, Ranieri needed persuading to sign him. He
didn't know much about Kanté and he confessed it was
Walsh who persistently urged him to see the deal through.
Walsh and his colleagues had put a lot of hours in research-
ing and analysing Kanté, and they were adamant he was the
real deal. Ranieri would admit later he was extremely grateful for Walsh's persistence.

AUGUST 2015

Before the 2015/16 season began, Leicester City were priced at 5000-1 to win the Premier League by the UK's biggest bookmakers, William Hill

ANTICIPATION AND TREPIDATION
IN EQUAL MEASURE

No matter what befalls a team during a football season, whether it turns out to be a season the supporters will never forget or one that they will try for ever after to erase from their memories, every football fan walks towards the ground on the opening day of the season full of hope and anticipation. No matter how bleak or successful the previous campaign may have been, even the most negative of supporters will have the thought in the back of their minds that this could be their season. It is a fresh start, a new beginning, a clean slate.

Of course, 90 minutes later that could all have changed and the pint pot half-empty brigade may have cast aside whatever optimism they felt at the start of the game.

Before the first fixture, even the doom merchants – and every club has more than their fair share of them – will feel a sense of optimism, although of course, they wouldn't admit it to anyone.

Those people are a strange breed; the anti-fan, as I like to call them. They never seem more happy than when they are miserable. When their team is struggling they are in their element. They renounce the club repeatedly, bemoan the players and the manager, and generally seem as though their chosen football club is the bane of their existence. Yet week after week they return, no matter how bad it gets. It is almost as if the football club provides some sort of emotional crutch for the anti-fan. Their life may be a disappointment to them, full of frustrations, difficulties and challenges, and their team provides therapy. They can release all that negative tension on a Saturday afternoon and direct it towards the pitch. Normally the protagonists who take the brunt are the officials, but often their own players and manager are the target. However, don't make the mistake of thinking they don't love their club. It is a love-hate relationship, as it often is with a sibling. The anti-fan is allowed to criticise and complain about his team, but watch how he springs to the club's defence if someone else dares to disparage them. He will defend them to the hilt.

Heading into Leicester City's opening game of the season, against Sunderland on 8 August at the King Power Stadium, there was plenty of optimism around the City camp.

It had been a short, if traumatic, summer for City and memories were still fresh of their 5-1 win over Queens Park Rangers on home soil just over two months before. It had been a glorious end to what had eventually turned out to be a memorable and successful season.

The bookmakers were not quite so optimistic with regard to City's chances. City were already among the favourites to be facing a relegation battle but the mixed reaction to Ranieri's appointment resulted in several of the bookies cutting the odds on City being relegated from 7/2 to 11/4 on the day Ranieri was appointed. As for their chances of winning the title, two bookmakers, William Hill and Ladbrokes were offering odds of 5,000-1. 5,000-1 in a 20-team race. It seemed ridiculous but that was how ridiculous the concept was of the Foxes winning the title.

Ranieri had seemed oblivious to any negativity emanating from outside the club during his first official pre-match press conference in the media suite at the King Power Stadium, the scene of so many memorable moments from the previous campaign, but he certainly knew what was being said about his appointment. He seemed to be on a charm offensive when he first walked into the room. There were plenty of cameras positioned on the stage at the back of the room and around 20 journalists in attendance, many of whom were about to watch Ranieri in 'media mode' for the first time. I had interviewed him pitchside during pre-season and found him very easy going, polite and professional, but he took it up another level with such a large audience in attendance.

It was the first time the media would see Ranieri's pre-conference ritual of walking around the room and shaking the hand of every person in attendance. It wasn't a one-off. In fact, he has carried out this ritual before every press conference since, even though as City's season has developed into such a remarkable story there have been twice the number of journalists attending. The handshakes can take almost as long as the actual questions. It is a simple touch but an extremely effective one as it is seen as Ranieri showing his respect to the journalists, many of whom were expecting to have to write some pretty negative things about this man in the future. Any such criticism would have been much more vicious in nature had not the general consensus been, from that moment on, that Ranieri was a gentleman. Journalists can be pretty ruthless but how could you really stick the knife into someone who came across as so genteel and likeable?

Pre-season saw Ranieri slowly start to put his own stamp on City. He had started several of the games with the same wing-back system, with three centre-backs, that had served City so well in their Great Escape, but every time he had changed it back to a more conventional flat back four during the course of the game. In addition, there were also early signs of the counter-attacking style that City would hone to perfection, with Vardy being employed in his more natural central striking position and Mahrez on the right flank, enabling him to cut in on his favoured left foot.

City's starting line-up against the Black Cats had a very familiar feel to it, with just Okazaki of the completely new arrivals in the starting XI. Huth, also officially a new signing, would renew his partnership alongside Wes Morgan at the heart of the defence.

Morgan had been picked despite having had literally no pre-season. The Jamaica international had a very short holiday before returning to the club in the week before the campaign kicked off, having been on international duty with the Reggae Boyz at the Copa America in Chile and then the Concacaf Gold Cup in the United States and Canada. He had just two training sessions before the Sunderland game.

There had been real concern within the club of the physical demands that this would place on Morgan and what kind of shape he would be in when he returned for the new season. Pearson had tried to persuade him to choose just one tournament, but Morgan saw the summer as an opportunity he didn't want to miss at this stage of his career. He would go on to play every minute of every league game in 2015/16.

Like so many of his City teammates, Morgan's passage into the professional game had not been entirely smooth. City would be dubbed 'The Misfits' by the media during the campaign as they had nearly all faced adversity or rejection at some point in their careers. For Morgan it came when he was 15. He had come from a tough area of Nottingham, The Meadows. He could have been led down the wrong path, but he had football. He would admit that a lot of the people he knew from his childhood had ended up in jail, but he was protected from that fate because of his involvement in the game. His family and his friends could see that football was his ticket out of a life that would consume so many around the area. However, he almost packed it all in. He was rejected at the age of 15 by Notts County and his dream seemed to be over. He played briefly for Dunkirk, a non-league side in Nottingham, but there was no hiding from the fact that his dream of making a living out of football might not happen.

But then Nottingham Forest picked him up. Even then, manager Paul Hart confessed he didn't think he was fit enough to be a professional but Forest staff, convinced of Morgan's ability, would train him in secret to get him in shape before Hart saw him again. After promising performances in the youth team, he was offered a professional contract and made his debut in the first team at the age of 19. He would go on to be Forest's longest-serving player. He spent a decade at the club, in which time Forest managed to climb out of League One and back to the Championship, but there didn't seem to be a realistic opportunity for Morgan to fulfil his dream of playing in the Premier League.

It wasn't all about the money for Morgan. He wasn't on big money at Forest but had begun to grow uneasy with the fact that several fringe players at Forest were earning considerably more than him and when he was made his last contract offer he was unhappy with the terms. Leicester also offered Morgan a more realistic chance of promotion and in 2012 he joined in a £1 million deal. He was soon made club captain and led City to the Championship title. His dream to play in the Premier League had become reality.

Such struggles were a common theme among the City players. 'I am sure there are players out there who have come from a lot of different backgrounds and different career paths but I think this group of players, definitely we have been together for a while and have gone through a lot,' said Morgan. 'We have got promoted from the Championship and avoided relegation against all odds. We have a real belief and togetherness; we are like a family. A few players have joined our team and just bought into the philosophy of how we are as a team. We get on so well. We do things on and off the pitch. There is that real togetherness about us all and it all goes together and bodes well for when we go out there on the pitch; we all fight and we all want to go that extra yard and push ourselves as far as possible.'

He was also invited to represent Jamaica and with any hopes of an England call-up looking unlikely he seized the chance to experience international football – so why wouldn't he have wanted to head to Chile, to face some of the most high-profile strikers in the world in Uruguay's Edison Cavani, Paraguay's Roque Santa Cruz and Argentina's Lionel Messi, Ángel Di María and Gonzalo Higuaín? Afterwards, he headed north for the Gold Cup and helped Jamaica reach the final, only to lose to Mexico in Philadelphia. It was an unbelievable, unmissable experience for Morgan, and a long way from The Meadows. It was the football equivalent of 'live while you're alive and sleep when you're dead'.

It was a summer to remember for Morgan, but for his City teammate Marc Albrighton it had been a very different, and extremely difficult, close season.

Albrighton had endured a challenging first season as a City player. He had spent his entire career up to that point with Aston Villa, the club he had idolised growing up. He joined Villa as an eight-year-old and had worked his way through the ranks to break into the first team as a 19-year-old. His career at Villa had been on an upward trajectory until he fell out of favour under Paul Lambert and he was shocked to discover at the end of the 2013/14 season that he was being released, despite having been told he would get a new deal. He would state that he didn't even get a call from Lambert to wish him good luck when he left.

The start of his City career hadn't gone much better and he was used mainly as a substitute for the majority of the season, much to his frustration, until he came on as a half-time substitute against West Ham United and helped City to a win that triggered their phenomenal run to secure safety. He was then an ever-present during the Great Escape and would prove to be an integral part of Ranieri's side.

However, he and his family suffered personal pain during the summer as the mother of his partner Chloe Fulford, Sue Davey, and her partner Scott Chalkley, were among the 38 victims of the Sousse terrorist attacks in Tunisia on 26 June. It was testament to Albrighton's professionalism that he was back for the first day of pre-season training shortly afterwards and he lined up with the rest of his City teammates against the Black Cats for the season opener at the King Power Stadium. He would be a key figure in the match.

Albrighton was the provider for City's first two goals as he teed up Vardy and then Mahrez with trademark curling free-kicks and crosses inside the first 18 minutes. Mahrez was then tripped inside the area by Lee Cattermole, who had a dreadful first 30 minutes and was swiftly withdrawn after Mahrez had fired City into a three-goal lead.

Jermain Defoe, who had chosen Sunderland over Leicester in the previous January transfer window, pulled a goal back for the visitors before Albrighton restored City's three-goal lead and despite Steven Fletcher pulling another goal back for the Black Cats, City had got off to a comfortable start.

LEICESTER MERCURY BLOG, 12 AUGUST 2015
CITY GET OFF TO A FLIER

Last Saturday's opening-day victory over Sunderland was a fantastic start for Leicester City.

But while it was a great morale booster after the uncertainty created by this summer's events, I am sure no one around City is getting too carried away.

For a start I doubt City will face another side as bad as Sunderland in the Premier League this season. They were truly horrendous. Yes, you can justifiably argue City made them look bad with the intensity and commitment they displayed, but the fact is the Black Cats were simply woeful.

City could have won by an even greater margin and should have taken more of the many excellent chances they created, while they will be very disappointed by the two goals they conceded.

There will be much tougher challenges ahead, starting this Saturday at West Ham United who are buoyant after their impressive opening display at Arsenal.

However, the positives far outweighed the negatives and the front four of Vardy, Okazaki, Albrighton and Mahrez looked quick, sharp and hungry, and any defence in the division will now be aware of them.

Danny Drinkwater and Andy King also allayed any fears about the impact of the departure of Esteban Cambiasso and Matty James's knee injury.

The Blue Army also demonstrated their determination to continue those fantastic home atmospheres which contributed so much to the Great Escape at the end of the last season. That will be a crucial factor this season.

Claudio Ranieri couldn't have asked for a better start. The Italian will continue to have his sceptics for now but if

City continue to put in exhilarating performances like last Saturday then the doubters will be silenced.

City still need to bring in some new bodies in my opinion, especially to provide even more quality in the crucial midfield engine room, but work is afoot to do just that and over the next couple of weeks I suspect City fans will see a couple of new arrivals if City can land their targets.

All in all, it was a good opening day to the season with plenty of exciting football and a few shocks along the way, illustrating the continued competitive nature of the Premier League and why it is such a global spectacle.

After the game Albrighton came through the Mixed Zone, where journalists wait to try to stop players to ask them about the game. He knew he was going to be asked about the death of his fiancée's mother in the terror attacks, at a time when the wounds were still open and raw, but he knew it was an opportunity to thank the supporters and everyone else who had offered their condolences. He faced the media with dignity. Those he had lost would have been proud. Albrighton is a class act, on and off the pitch.

'If I can play football then it is taking my mind off things and if I am doing well my family are happy and that is all I can ask for,' he said. 'I will see them now and they will all be happy; when you see them smiling it is the best thing in the world.'

Not all players are happy to stop in the Mixed Zone, regardless of which club they play for. Some never do. Some walk through holding their phone to their ear, pretending to talk. Some choose selective deafness and completely ignore the pleas of the journalists, while some overseas players pretend their excellent English isn't quite as good as it has previously been. Some are just downright rude. The journalists have a saying for it. It is called getting 'pied off' when a player blanks you or refuses a request for a quick chat. I have taken my fair share of custard pies over the years.

There is a brilliant quote from the film *Jerry Maguire* which sums it up. In a scene when Tom Cruise's sports agent is trying to explain to his one and only client, Cuba Gooding Jr's character Rod Tidwell, what it is like trying to negotiate on his behalf, he describes it as 'a pride-swallowing siege'. That is the best description of what it is like sometimes to be a football journalist. You have to be prepared to swallow your pride a lot. You have to accept that you are not in the dominant position, that you are reliant on the goodwill of the individuals to stop and speak. They are under no obligation, although I have often wondered why it is such an effort for some to stop for three minutes before heading home. I always tell the players who are prepared to listen that ultimately they are not talking to me, they are talking to the fans, offering them their thoughts on the game and the season ahead. How much of a chore is it really?

I have never had a custard pie from Albrighton. It may be because I am a fellow Tamworthian and was the sports editor of the *Tamworth Herald* when we followed his rise through the Villa ranks. Local boy makes good stories are the meat and drink of local newspapers, and we carried plenty of Albrighton stories.

In truth, though, it is because Albrighton is a genuinely decent guy who understands that not only are the journalists just trying to do their job but that modern football is built on the devotion of the supporters through their ticket purchases and satellite television subscriptions. The media is a huge part of football and the players are handsomely rewarded for the attention. Albrighton gets it.

It was a sombre moment but it didn't detract from what had been an excellent first day back at the office for City.

OKAZAKI BURSTS HAMMERS' BUBBLES

The Boleyn Ground has not been a happy hunting ground for Leicester City. In fact, it would be fair to say City fans will be glad to see the back of the place as prior to 2015/16 their side had tasted success there just once since 1966. In 2000 Darren Eadie had been the last Leicester player to score a winner at West Ham since Hammers heroes Bobby Moore, Geoff Hurst and Martin Peters won the World Cup for England. So the optimism was tinged with apprehension as City headed along Green Street for the last time before the Hammers switched to the more palatial surroundings of the Olympic Stadium.

The Boleyn Ground was one of the last few traditional footballing cathedrals left. It is a unique ground, steeped in history and nostalgia. With the nearby flats towering over the East Stand and the pre-match bubbles floating down from the West Stand, there is something special about the Boleyn Ground.

However, the atmosphere outside the ground is one of the most intimidating in English football. On several occasions while walking down from Upton Park station I have seen trouble and it is one of those areas where you make sure you keep your head down and don't look anyone directly in the eye, for fear they will instantly recognise you are not from their 'manor'.

My caution is born out of experience of seeing what could happen to those who are not quite so careful, so I genuinely feared for a small group of City fans who jumped on to a packed tube to Upton Park and proceeded to perform their repertoire of City songs, some of which were directly aimed at Hammers fans. There were only three of them and they didn't look like they were out of their teens, so it was youthful bravado in the extreme. Some fellow passengers, who were non-football commuters, asked them to pipe down, which only made them sing louder. Their intention was obviously to annoy.

But it was the Hammers fans who started looking down the train and talking quietly among themselves, with their eyes constantly locked on the trio, that caught my eye and at the next stop I jumped off and moved a few carriages down. I didn't want to get caught up in any nonsense. I was there to work and didn't want to spend the afternoon instead helping police with their enquiries.

Fortunately for the three boys nothing did happen in the carriage, but they carried on pushing their luck as they moved off the station platform. The police had now spotted them too. It was hard to miss them as they continued singing anti-Hammers songs, and several officers moved to follow them as they headed out on to Green Street, primarily for the boys' own safety, I imagined.

Still, I could see several little groups of Hammers fans looking down the road after them, gesturing to one another as if communicating in a secret code, but the boys carried on completely oblivious. It was like watching a wildlife show where the prey is slowly being stalked by the predators. I couldn't watch any more as the pack seemed to be closing in for the kill, so I moved very quickly to get into the ground. At several points that afternoon I wondered what happened to those boys and whether what little sense they seemed to possess was knocked out of them at some point.

The Hammers also had a new man in charge, Slaven Bilić. The charismatic, guitar-playing Croatian was a hero at the Boleyn Ground from his brief stint there as a player, in complete contrast to his predecessor Sam Allardyce, who had never won the majority of the Hammers faithful over, despite moderate success – although their qualification for the Europa League had come through the Fair Play table.

The qualifying rounds for the European competition had meant an early start for the Hammers. They had kicked-off their season on 2 July and had already played seven games before the Foxes' visit. They had demonstrated on the opening day of the season that they were ahead of their Premier League rivals in terms of fitness and match sharpness with a 2-0 win at Arsenal, adding to the sense that City would have their work cut out if their poor record at the Boleyn Ground wasn't to be extended.

At the heart of City's performance was little Japanese international Shinji Okazaki. He had made a reasonable debut the week before, but now really showed the City fans why Pearson had been scouting him for well over a year before spending £7 million for his services. Like most Japanese players, what he lacked in physical stature he more than made up for with heart and desire.

He wasn't the first Japan international to sign for City. Paulo Sousa had recruited defensive midfielder Yuki Abe in 2010 and he was exactly the same as Okazaki in many ways. Abe was incredibly hardworking as a player and very likeable as a person. He was always polite, courteous and respectful, and extremely generous with his time with journalists and supporters alike. Abe never really settled at City. He was popular with the other players and forged an unlikely friendship with goalkeeper Chris Weale, but his lack of English made integration difficult and he was homesick. Unlike Okazaki, Abe had never played outside of Japan before he came to England. When Nigel Pearson returned to the club he agreed to cancel Abe's contract so he could return to Urawa Red Diamonds in his homeland.

The Japanese journalists who are employed solely to follow the few Japanese players in England around the country said Okazaki was different to Abe. He was more of a 'lad' – and he is certainly more outgoing, as the video of his initiation ceremony in Austria proved, as he belted out a karaoke tune with gusto. His time in Germany with Mainz had helped Okazaki adjust to a change in culture and he certainly embraced his new environment well.

While the rest of us would find it difficult to get certain players to stop to chat for just a couple of minutes after games, Okazaki would come through and stop for up to 20 minutes talking to the Japanese journalists. Even if he hadn't played, he was there for an interview. He knew this small group of journalists were following City around the country just to speak to him afterwards and he never let them down. He showed them respect.

Quite often the rest of us in the press pack would wonder what on earth there was left to talk about as the conversations would drag on, but after City's 2-1 win at West Ham Okazaki had plenty to talk about because he had a fine game. He had opened the scoring after 27 minutes when he bundled the ball home after Adrián had saved his initial effort from Vardy's cross. He showed great tenacity to latch on to the rebound before the recovering Hammers defenders could get back and it would become an Okazaki trademark goal.

Mahrez followed up his double against Sunderland on the opening day by scoring City's second 11 minutes later to burst the bubbles of the home fans, with Albrighton providing the assist. It would not be the last time the two would combine so effectively.

Predictably, the Hammers fought back, with Dimitri Payet scoring ten minutes after the interval but City held on to make it only the second time they had started a Premier League campaign with back-to-back wins. The other was the 1997/98 season when City picked up eight points from their first four games. Ranieri's City would soon match that achievement, and then eclipse it.

LEICESTER MERCURY BLOG, 19 AUGUST 2015
TINKERING WITH A SMALL 'T'

It was hailed as the return to the Premier League of 'the Tinkerman' but so far Claudio Ranieri is not living up to that reputation.

And that appears to be good news for all concerned.

Ranieri appears to enjoy the tag and declared to the media after Saturday's win at West Ham United that he was the flag-bearer for all Tinkermen, the pioneer for Tinkerers, but he has been wise enough to leave so much about City well alone and only make minor changes.

It is fair to say that his appointment as Nigel Pearson's successor received a mixed response from City fans, if postings on websites and social media are a good indicator, although sometimes they certainly are not.

I suspect the fear was the Tinkerman would come in and rip up the foundations that have been laid over the past three years and dismantle a squad full of promising young players that was expected to just keep getting better after the upturn in form at the end of the last campaign.

That fear has proven to be unfounded.

Ranieri has said straight from the off that he doesn't intend to change too much and he has been true to his word in many respects.

The existing coaching staff are still in place and influencing proceedings as much as before, with Craig Shakespeare very visible in the technical area at West Ham United alongside Ranieri.

He has brought in some of his own coaching staff but there has been no disruption to the status quo.

The recruitment policy has remained consistent with players City have identified for some time as targets still on the radar and in the case of N'Golo Kanté, Ranieri appears to be more than happy to follow the judgement of Steve Walsh, who has an excellent record for spotting young talent across Europe.

You only have to look at the way Riyad Mahrez's stock is rising in the Premier League for evidence of that fact.

On the pitch there has been a change in system, but it appears to be the traditional 4-4-2 formation that City employed on a regular basis under Pearson.

A front two; two wide men, one willing to come inside into central areas while the other loves to stay wide and whip in dangerous crosses; two sitting midfielders backed up by an established back four.

Sound familiar?

But that basic assessment doesn't tell the whole story, according to the players I have spoken to over the past couple of weeks.

I have asked both Marc Albrighton and Andy King if anything has changed because from the outside it seems like business as usual, and while both admitted there has been a stability and continuity about Ranieri's transition, they said Ranieri has left his mark on the side.

Neither would go into too much detail, not wishing to inadvertently give away any trade secrets, but both mentioned the way the side is set up and organised as a difference.

Obviously, it is very early days and no one is getting too carried away by City's excellent start to the season, but judging by both opening performances there does seem to be a distinct structure to how City have gone about their play.

King and Danny Drinkwater have gone forward on occasions, and both have had excellent chances to get on the scoresheet, but their role has been to provide the side's insurance policy, always ready to step in and cover the front four who have launched what are rapidly becoming City's trademark lightning counter-attacks.

In both games the opposition have had more possession of the ball and it appears City are happy to stay organised and patient, waiting for the opportunity to break quickly with Albrighton, Mahrez, Jamie Vardy and Shinji Okazaki, all of whom have a good turn of pace and a directness to their play.

City were more effective as a counter-attacking side under Pearson, but it is a subtle change to City's approach under Ranieri.

It is tinkering from the Tinkerman with a small 't'.

One big difference though is the contrast in Ranieri's public persona and private managerial style.

While Pearson often appeared bristling and difficult in public while dealing with the media, he was not the bullish character in the dressing room.

Occasionally he would strip the walls with a verbal blast if required but in general he preferred to stay calm and get his point across in a methodical fashion.

Ranieri is the opposite. He is a real gentleman publicly, starting every pre-match press conference by shaking every journalist's hand while every question is answered politely and with a sense of humour.

However, more than one person at City says that Ranieri has already shown his emotional, Italian side by venting his frustration forcibly if his instructions are not carried out to his liking.

The Tinkerman has teeth.

THE CHAMPION AND THE STREET KID

Claudio Ranieri had finally found his 'champion'.

Since the departure of Esteban Cambiasso in July, City fans had been waiting with bated breath to see who Ranieri would bring in to replace the Argentinian. Expectations were high. The signing of Cambiasso a year before had raised the benchmark for City signings. It was impossible to find someone with the same pedigree as Cambiasso, but the signing of Gökhan Inler from Napoli drew a positive response.

City had looked around before plumping for the Switzerland captain. Chile international midfielder Charles Aránguiz was reportedly a target but he opted to join Bundesliga side Bayer Leverkusen. City were believed to have agreed a fee of £10.5 million with the midfielder's Brazilian club Internacional but the lure of Champions League football with Leverkusen convinced Aránguiz to head to Germany.

Inler was the fifth most capped player by his country, a veteran of over 80 international games. He had won the Swiss Super League twice and spent eight years in Italy with Udinese and then Napoli. He had won the Italian Super Cup during four years in Naples before deciding to try his luck in the Premier League after City agreed a £5 million fee.

Other Premier League clubs had tried to sign Inler, with West Ham United said to be one, and he revealed he had offers from abroad too, but had plumped for City. City were expected to be battling for Premier League survival again and Inler said he was up for the fight. He had developed a love of boxing while in Italy and regularly sparred with former Italian, European and World WBA light welterweight champion Patrizio Oliva; he believed the noble art would help him handle the physicality of his new challenge, but it was the relentless pace of the English game and City's lightning-quick, Blitzkrieg attacking style that would prove the biggest challenge to Inler.

Inler held court with the media in the build-up to City's second home game of the campaign, the visit of Tottenham Hotspur, and he came across as a confident and relaxed individual. But would he prove to be the on-field leader that Cambiasso had been? City fans hoped so.

However, it was to be a more familiar face that would prove to be City's star man against a rapidly improving young Spurs side being well marshalled by Mauricio Pochettino: Riyad Mahrez. Mahrez had started the season in sensational form, scoring three times in the first two games, and he added to his tally with a superb individual strike which cancelled out Dele Alli's goal for Spurs just a minute before, which had come against the run of play.

Mahrez had been discovered while playing for Le Havre in Ligue 2. The City scouts had actually been there to watch Ryan Mendes playing for opponents Lille, but it was the diminutive but waspish forward Mahrez who captured their attention. City snapped him up for the modest fee of £400,000 in January, 2014. (Mendes would soon go on to follow Mahrez to England, signing for City's East Midlands rivals Nottingham Forest.) Following the success of another young French-based player, Anthony Knockaert, City fans hoped Mahrez would prove another gem.

At first it took Mahrez time to adjust to the physicality of the English game, as well as the tactical and defensive demands of Nigel Pearson, but he would play a valuable part in City's Championship title success and his performances would earn him a call-up to the Algeria squad, the country of his father's birth.

Pearson and his staff rated Mahrez highly. While Knockaert was the fans' favourite, the coaches always thought Mahrez had the potential to be even better. They had worked on him physically but what had been impressive, and what came to the fore during his first season in the Premier League, was Mahrez's mental strength. What he may have lacked in physical strength he more than made up for in character. Bravery in football comes in many forms. Traditionally in England the players who fly into tackles or put their head in where the boots are flying are considered the brave ones, but it is equally brave, if not more so, to keep wanting the ball in pressure situations. Even if Mahrez lost the ball, and the groans would emanate from the stands, he would want to get possession back as quickly as possible and try again. He wouldn't hide on the flanks or play the simple pass every time; even if things weren't going his way, he would try different ways to open up a defence, whether that meant running at a defender or trying a trick to beat an opponent.

Mahrez is a supremely confident player with a unique style, a technique that wasn't coached in any academy, as has become the norm these days. Mahrez developed his skills playing on the suburban streets of Paris, and his mental strength came from his upbringing. As back stories go, Mahrez's rise is as impressive as that of any of his City teammates, who all seem to have risen to the Premier League the hard way.

He was born in Sarcelles, a northern suburb of the French capital and a commune for so many settlers from Algeria who moved to France during the Algerian War of Independence. His upbringing there was humble, but Mahrez would state that he never wanted for anything. He was extremely close to his father, Ahmed, who encouraged his football and pushed him to become a professional.

Ahmed had been a player himself in the lower leagues of Algeria and then France, and he was Mahrez's inspiration, until his sudden death when Mahrez was just 15 years old. Mahrez has spoken publicly about how devastating the loss was, but how it spurred him on to try to make his father's dream come true.

'It was difficult, life. I am not going to say I was poor. I wasn't rich or poor. Life was normal. I didn't want for any-thing,' said Mahrez. 'When my dad died it was difficult. He was encouraging me and behind me, giving me advice. That is why I am here now. I hope he is happy. My mum was alone after he died and it was difficult but that has helped me to be stronger. That is maybe why I am the man I am now. When your dad dies it is normal to take on more responsibility because your mum is alone. In our culture the man is the boss of the house so I took on more responsibility and I still have. I am proud of that.'

He was playing for his local team, Sarcelles, but the big clubs were not interested in him. Despite his obvious skil-ful qualities, they told him he was too skinny to be able to cope with the physical demands of professional football. Mahrez was not deterred, displaying the belligerence and single-mindedness that would serve him so well in later years. He may not have had the physique, but he certainly had the character, as his former technical director at Sarcelles, Mohamed Coulibaly, told French national newspaper *L'Equipe* in 2014.

'He was very frail, but he never gave up and that's paying off,' said Coulibaly. 'You can see on the pitch that he never hides. From very early on he learned to take responsibilities. He has something more than technique, he has the guts and character that make great players.'

In 2009 Quimper, a team in the fourth tier of French football, took a chance on him. He caught the eye of Paris Saint-Germain, but chose to join Le Havre, in the French second division, instead. Joining in 2010, he played for their under-21s and reserves. He also signed his first professional contract when he was 19, fulfilling his father's dream. He eventually progressed to the first team where his skills would soon attract the attention of City's head of recruitment, Steve Walsh, the man who had developed a knack of unearthing hidden gems.

Mahrez's performances during his first season in the Premier League, especially towards the end, led to specu-lation that bigger clubs were now paying more attention to him. His performances for Algeria at the 2014 World Cup increased the spotlight on him, prompting City to sign him to a new four-year contract until 2019. Now the skinny kid from Sarcelles was playing football on some of the biggest stages in the world, both domestically in the Premier League and internationally.

He had faced obstacles and overcome them, but now there was another set before him. His goals in the first three games of the season demonstrated that he was a match-winner, one of City's biggest attacking threats, and he would have to deal with the extra attention he would receive from defenders. A week after his stunning strike against

Tottenham Hotspur, Leicester headed to AFC Bournemouth and Mahrez was withdrawn by Ranieri at half-time. He had put the ball in the net early on, but was flagged for a marginal offside and after that he was stifled by the close attentions of the Cherries defenders, taking a heavy tackle early on which certainly slowed him down. It was a minor setback; despite the extra attention and occasional heavy treatment he was now attracting, he would not be suppressed for long.

THE COMEBACK KINGS AND
THE CANNON STARTS TO FIRE

Claudio Ranieri's men were proving tough to beat. In fact, they were becoming a side that didn't know when they were beaten.

They had come from behind against Spurs to remain unbeaten and had done so again at Bournemouth. Trailing to Callum Wilson's spectacular first-half goal at the Vitality Stadium, City had huffed and puffed on the south coast in search of an equaliser, but one was not forthcoming until Jamie Vardy drove at the Cherries defence with five minutes remaining and drew a foul from Steve Cook. With designated penalty taker Mahrez off the pitch, Vardy stepped up himself to smash the spot-kick home. Vardy wheeling away in delight would become a familiar sight over the coming weeks.

AUGUST SUMMARY

Competition	Date	Fixture
Premier League	Sat 8 Aug	Leicester 4-2 Sunderland
Premier League	Sat 15 Aug	West Ham 1-2 Leicester
Premier League	Sat 22 Aug	Leicester 1-1 Tottenham
League Cup – Second Round	Tue 25 Aug	Bury 1-4 Leicester
Premier League	Sat 29 Aug	Bournemouth 1-1 Leicester

*By the end of August Leicester's odds had shortened
to 2500-1 (William Hill, 5 September 2015)*

SEPTEMBER 2015

		P	W	D	L	GF	GA	GD	Pts
1	Manchester City	4	4	0	0	10	0	10	12
2	Crystal Palace	4	3	0	1	8	5	3	9
3	Leicester City	4	2	2	0	8	5	3	8
4	Swansea City	4	2	2	0	7	4	3	8

Standings on 1 September

As the transfer window closed last night there will be fans up and down the country questioning if their clubs have done enough business.

As spending during the summer hit a new record of £870 million, £1 billion for the calendar year including the last January window, supporters will also be wondering if their club has invested wisely or just thrown away the cash and panic bought as the window closed.

With the television deal increasing from the current £3.018 billion to an eye-watering £5.136 billion over three years from next season, it is obvious why so many clubs aspiring to stay in the division have decided to splash the cash.

The most active were new boys Watford with an incredible 15 new players arriving at Vicarage Road for a gross spend of £33 million, while Bournemouth spent £19 million on 12 players, although the third promoted side, Norwich, signed just five players with an estimated spend of £10 million.

At the other end of the scale, Manchester City spent £154.2 million, a net spend of £101.3 million, and broke their transfer record twice, on Raheem Sterling and Kevin De Bruyne, as they bid to wrestle the title back off Chelsea and stay ahead of their equally big-spending city rivals, who spent £115 million.

Leicester City have spent an estimated £25 million on seven new players as they look to build on their outstanding form towards the back end of last season and their excellent start to this campaign.

Despite having picked up a possible 29 points from 13 games since 1 April there was still a need to bolster a squad that had struggled so badly for two thirds of last season and lost influential player of the year Esteban Cambiasso during the summer.

In my opinion, City have done decent business during the window but are still very much reliant on the players who came to the fore towards the end of the last campaign.

The £3 million signing of Robert Huth from Stoke was crucial. Along with Cambiasso, Huth had the biggest impact on City during his loan spell in the second half of last season and his permanent arrival was crucial to offset the disappointment of Cambiasso's decision to leave.

Full-back Christian Fuchs was a free signing from German side Schalke and he brings plenty of experience as the captain of Austria, as well as his appearances in the Champions League.

At 29 years old he should also be in the prime of his career, but the departure of Nigel Pearson, the man who convinced Fuchs to join City, has raised question marks over whether new boss Claudio Ranieri is a fan.

Fuchs has made one start so far, in the Capital One Cup, and had the least amount of pitch time during pre-season of any City outfield player. He currently appears to be back-up to Jeff Schlupp.

City spent £7 million on Japan international Shinji Okazaki, a player Pearson had been tracking for at least a year, and he does appear to have impressed Ranieri, starting three of City's opening four Premier League games.

Okazaki's work rate and commitment is similar to that of Jamie Vardy and the early signs are the pair could form a strong partnership. The question is will they score enough goals?

City made a failed £12 million offer for Charlie Austin during the summer and his arrival would have given City even more firepower. It remains surprising that Austin, who still scored 18 Premier League goals in a relegated Queens Park Rangers side last season, wasn't snapped up, although there were reports he rejected a move to Crystal Palace.

N'Golo Kanté is another player who has been lively since his arrival and at £5.6 million the little Frenchman looks like a terrier of a midfielder. He was never meant to be a replacement for Cambiasso, but is certainly a player with plenty of potential. The question mark with Kanté is how quickly will he settle and adapt to life in the Premier League? He may be one for the future.

Yohan Benalouane was recruited to bolster the back four, especially after Matt Upson was allowed to leave. City fans have not seen a lot of Benalouane so far, except for his appearance in the Capital One Cup at Bury and a couple of substitute appearances.

He appears to be a strong and uncompromising defender, but in his few appearances he appears to have a tendency to make rash challenges and the number of bookings he could potentially pick up would be a concern unless he adapts his game.

City fans were crying out for a midfielder to arrive at the club with an international stature and reputation following Cambiasso's departure.

Switzerland international Gökhan Inler was the leader Ranieri identified and he managed to land the 31-year-old for £5 million from Napoli.

The early season form of Andy King and Danny Drinkwater has meant City fans have not seen much of Inler so far but a lot will be expected from him as the season goes on. He has big shoes to fill in central midfield.

Finally, it was evident after the season started and when Ranieri opted for a more orthodox 4-4-2 that City needed cover and competition in wide positions for Riyad Mahrez and Marc Albrighton.

There were certainly a number of contenders, with bids being submitted for Demarai Gray at Birmingham City and Peru international André Carrillo at Sporting Lisbon, without success.

Ahmed Elmohamady at Hull City was also on the radar, as were a number of others who remained undisclosed, I am sure.

But on deadline day City landed Nathan Dyer on a season-long loan, and this could be a shrewd piece of business.

Gray would have cost at least £5 million but while he is a promising player, he is not the finished article and would have taken time to develop, possibly even out on loan.

Carrillo has pedigree and is an exciting player, but at over £9 million, which it may have taken to land the 24-year-old, City would have taken a big risk on him being able to adapt to the Premier League.

It was obviously a risk they decided not to take for now as they didn't offer any more than the reported £8.8 million they submitted as a second bid.

Elmohamady has Premier League experience and is versatile enough to play anywhere down the right-hand side, but City were put off by Hull's asking price.

But Dyer ticks all the boxes. His deal is relatively cheap, he is still only 27 years old, he has performed to a good level in the Premier League for Swansea, is still hungry for success and offers something different to what City have at their disposal currently.

Whereas Mahrez likes to come in off his flank and Albrighton likes to find space to whip in early crosses, Dyer is a more orthodox winger who loves to take on full-backs.

City could have done more in the window, certainly, and

there were a few deals that weren't possible to do which would have excited the fans, like Austin and Carrillo.

But if the remit was to strengthen the squad rather than completely overhaul it then City appear to have done just that.

Of course, the biggest aspect now is how Ranieri gets them performing to their best abilities.

That is the real acid test of how successful City have been in the transfer window.

Vardy's pace and movement down the middle had proved so effective in the opening games of the season and had earned him another call-up to the England squad for the European Championship qualifiers away at San Marino and against Inler's Switzerland at Wembley. Vardy was given his first England start in San Marino, completing his mesmeric rise from factory worker and part-time footballer to an England starter, but the pride was tinged with a little frustration as Vardy was utilised in a wide role by England manager Roy Hodgson.

Nigel Pearson had often employed Vardy as a wide striker in the past and at no point had the move ever looked effective. It restricted the areas Vardy could run into and made it easier for defenders to track his runs. When used down the middle he was proving to be a nightmare to deal with as invariably defenders didn't know where he would pop up. His former strike partner David Nugent, who had forged a great understanding with Vardy during the Championship title charge, had revealed Vardy was known within the City dressing room as 'the Cannon', as in 'loose cannon' because his behaviour was so unpredictable. That may have been a reference to his live-wire, prankster persona off the pitch but it was equally apt to describe his performances on it.

However, stuck out on the left flank in San Marino, Vardy's strengths were nullified, and not because of the ability of the part-time defenders: just the shackles placed upon him by Hodgson. In the end it seemed the frustration showed as Vardy ended up embroiled in his own personal feud with San Marino defender Giovanni Bonini.

Vardy had admitted it was a dream come true just to play for England but to do so at Wembley would be the pinnacle of his career to date. He would have to be patient on that score as he was an unused substitute in the 2-0 win over Switzerland a few days later, but it was still an historic night as Wayne Rooney scored to become England's all-time record goalscorer as Hodgson's men booked a place at the Euro 2016 finals in France.

The fact that a Leicester player was in the England reckoning again for the first time since Ian Walker in 2004 meant that I got the chance to head down Wembley Way myself to cover an England international. The fact Inler was captain of the Swiss sealed the deal as well.

When I had seen Vardy, following his initial call-up at the end of the previous season at St George's Park, he had looked happy to see a familiar face. He was being led by the England press officer to meet the national press and must have been nervous.

'I have warned them, I have a tendency to swear,' he said.

'Don't worry, just be yourself,' was the advice I offered. As if Vardy could be anything else.

This time the shoe was on the other foot as I waited in the Mixed Zone in the basement of Wembley. He hadn't played but he still came through to chat to me and the Leicester City media staff who had also made the journey.

He was obviously a little frustrated at not having made his Wembley debut and there must have been the fear that he might not get another chance, but the form he would continue in for City would ensure he would get the call from Hodgson again, and this time he would get to run out on the hallowed turf, coming on as a late substitute for Theo Walcott in the 2-0 win against Estonia in October, and then earning a fourth cap against Lithuania, although again he wasn't used in his preferred central position.

Back with City after the international break, Vardy was to continue where he left off at Bournemouth, and City would find themselves drawing on their considerable powers of recovery to keep their unbeaten start to the season going and set new club records. Aston Villa were the visitors to the King Power Stadium. They had won away at Bournemouth on the opening day of the season but had struggled to follow that up, so it was a major shock when they raced into a 2-0 lead. Jack Grealish and Carles Gil had put Villa in control with 27 minutes remaining and City looked to be heading for a first defeat of the season. What followed was incredible as City, who had looked so lifeless in the first half, sprang to life to claim a famous victory. Ritchie De Laet started the ball rolling with a header from a corner before Vardy swept home the equaliser from Danny Drinkwater's cross in the 82nd minute and with just a minute remaining Nathan Dyer, making his debut following his loan switch from Swansea City, headed home the winner to spark incredible scenes inside the King Power Stadium.

Supporter Liaison and Disability Access Officer, Jim Donnelly, was caught on camera celebrating wildly after Vardy's goal went in and the footage went viral on the internet, but Donnelly's chest-beating, fist-clenching, air-thumping jubilation was just typical of the feeling around the ground.

'I know I should show more decorum as I am working for the club on the day but I just can't help myself,' he told the *Mercury*. 'The lads had come back from the dead at 2-0 and levelled it. I just exploded with raw emotion. Nobody at the club has asked me to tone it down, so I won't. Anyway I couldn't if I tried. I wear my heart on my sleeve and I love Leicester City with all my heart.'

LEICESTER MERCURY BLOG, 16 SEPTEMBER 2015
MORE TO COME FROM INLER

Esteban Cambiasso was always going to be a tough act to follow.

His impact during the second half of last season will be forever cherished by City fans.

It will even take on folklore status.

In fact I can imagine young City fans now will be telling their kids in the future that they were there when Cambiasso scored that stunning goal against West Ham United to trigger a victory which kick-started City's Great Escape.

Or they will regale their offspring with tales of how the balding Argentinian would marshal his City teammates like a puppet master would at a seaside Punch and Judy show.

But what they probably won't say is that it took several months for Cambiasso to come to terms with the pace and physical demands of the Premier League, or how he was either a substitute or substituted until November last year.

The most decorated man in Argentine football history needed time to adjust to the demands of the Premier League.

After coming from Serie A, where the game is played

pretty much at walking pace compared to here in England, former manager Nigel Pearson recognised that despite the fact Cambiasso was obviously a class act, he needed time to get up to speed.

Gökhan Inler needs exactly the same consideration.

Expectations are already high enough considering boss Claudio Ranieri said he was scouring the globe for a leader to replace Cambiasso.

Inler has fantastic pedigree and an equally impressive CV.

However, he needs time and patience, and City's fantastic start should provide that luxury.

Andy King can justifiably feel a little unfortunate to have made way for Inler to make his full league debut against Aston Villa last Sunday.

In my opinion, King has matured into a very unselfish but extremely effective Premier League midfielder.

The Wales international forged his reputation on being a goalscoring midfielder, but the question was always how effective he was when he wasn't scoring goals. How much influence did he have in games?

Over the past few seasons King has developed a more rounded game. He is a better player now than he has ever been.

I went to Wembley just over a week ago to watch Inler take on England and he looked a class act. He was composed, like he had all the time in the world. He never looked rushed or wasted a pass.

However, international football has a very different timing to the Premier League.

City have built a reputation for being a very effective counter-attacking side and the secret to that trait is the ability to get the ball as quickly as possible to the men that make that happen.

In City's case that is the wide players Riyad Mahrez and Marc Albrighton, plus the pacey front men Shinji Okazaki and Jamie Vardy.

However, Inler's distribution last Sunday was a little slower than was required for City to be effective, purely because of his Serie A background.

Given time I am convinced he will be a solid performer for City.

Having said that, N'Golo Kanté looks tailor-made for English football. He is a real live wire and I am genuinely excited to see what he can achieve in a City shirt.

The following week, at Stoke City, it was a similar story. The Potters looked to be heading towards a comfortable victory after Bojan and Jonathan Walters had put them two goals to the good inside the first 20 minutes but once again City responded, inspired by their supporters, who applauded them from the field at half-time despite the deficit. Claudio Ranieri made the tactical switch to bring on Marc Albrighton and move live wire N'Golo Kanté into central midfield at the expense of Gökhan Inler, who was showing that he would need time to adjust to the speed and intensity of English football.

Danny Drinkwater was tripped by Marko Arnautović to give Riyad Mahrez the opportunity to reduce the arrears from the penalty spot and then Vardy beat the Stoke offside trap to slot home the equaliser to record his third goal in as many games.

City were getting a reputation as comeback kings and Vardy was starting to show the same kind of goalscoring form that he had shown during City's Championship title success.

THE RISE OF RANIERI AND VARDY

City's unbeaten start to the season continued with victory over West Ham United in the Capital One Cup at the King Power Stadium. Ranieri made ten changes to the side that had drawn at Stoke, with Gökhan Inler the only starter at the Britannia Stadium to retain his place, although he had been substituted at half-time at Stoke following a poor first half.

Joe Dodoo continued his sensational start to his City career with the opening goal, making it four goals in just two appearances after his hat-trick on debut at Bury in the previous round, but following Mauro Zárate's first-half equaliser it took a winner from Andy King in the 116th minute to put City through to the next round. It was King who had scored the late winner over the Hammers at the King Power Stadium the previous season to kick-start the Great Escape and once again it was the Wales international who was Leicester's hero, sending the City fans home happy.

However, City suffered their first setback at home to Arsenal the following Saturday. They could have been three goals to the good early on as Jamie Vardy hit the post and struck the crossbar with a header, while Ritchie De Laet also had an effort cleared off the line. As it was, City had just Vardy's fifth goal of the season (equalling his tally for the entire previous campaign) to show for their early dominance when Theo Walcott outpaced City's back four to equalise before Alexis Sanchez scored a hat-trick as the Gunners exposed the Foxes' defensive frailties. Olivier Giroud added to Leicester's woes late on and the only real positive was the continued goalscoring form of Vardy, who grabbed a further consolation goal for Ranieri's men.

There was a feeling around the King Power Stadium that City had been exposed, that they had been shown how far behind the Premier League's elite they actually were, despite their positive start to the season.

The goal at the start of the season was simply survival, yet again. City fans didn't want to go through the nerve-shredding experience of last season, when relegation loomed following a similar bright start and that famous 5-3 win over Manchester United.

So far the Tinkerman had not lived up to his name. Despite his reputation for constantly changing his teams in the past, Ranieri had identified that there wasn't a massive amount that needed changing after City's fantastic end to the 2014/15 season, but after the defeat at the hands of the Gunners, City fans waited with bated breath to see how he would react when they travelled to Norwich City the following week. There didn't seem to be a lot that needed altering in attack as City looked a vibrant attacking force, but their defensive record was a concern. The five they had shipped against the Gunners took their tally to 14 goals conceded in the opening seven games of the season and only Sunderland, who had looked so dismal on the opening day of the season, had conceded more.

SEPTEMBER SUMMARY

Competition	Date	Fixture
Premier League	Sun 13 Sep	Leicester 3-2 Aston Villa
Premier League	Sat 19 Sep	Stoke 2-2 Leicester
League Cup – Third Round	Tue 22 Sep	Leicester 2-1 West Ham
Premier League	Sat 26 Sep	Leicester 2-5 Arsenal

*Having slipped down to seventh in the league, taking
four points from three games in September, Leicester's odds
returned to 5000-1 (William Hill, 3 October 2015)*

OCTOBER 2015

		P	W	D	L	GF	GA	GD	Pts
1	Manchester United	7	5	1	1	12	5	7	16
2	Manchester City	7	5	0	2	13	6	7	15
3	West Ham United	7	4	1	2	15	9	6	13
4	Arsenal	7	4	1	2	10	7	3	13
8	Leicester City	7	3	3	1	15	14	1	12

Standings on 1 October

All Leicester City supporters will be watching on Saturday when the team is announced to see exactly how manager Claudio Ranieri responds to last week's 5-2 home defeat to Arsenal.

On the one hand it was another whole-hearted, gutsy display from City and in an attacking sense they were exciting to watch.

On the other they were far too open and were picked off by Arsenal's greater quality.

So what does Ranieri do? Does he stick with the way City have been playing, draw on the fact that it was their first defeat of the season and forge ahead with the knowledge that this attacking intent will bring the points City need for survival, but at the price of the occasional heavy defeat?

Or does he tighten City up defensively and sacrifice some of that attacking potency with the view that more solidity will yield less excitement but more positive results?

While there is no question City must improve dramatically defensively, I hope he opts for the former because in terms of a spectacle, watching this City side is a real thrill.

It is not as though it hasn't brought rewards either. The defeat to Arsenal was only their second in 18 games in all competitions and City are still unbeaten in seven away games.

One option Ranieri may look at, which could provide a stronger defensive platform, would be to revert to the three centre-back, wing-back system that Nigel Pearson employed at the end of last season.

Robert Huth and Wes Morgan certainly looked more comfortable with the extra cover that system provided.

In the last few games City have been cut open far too easily by runners down the middle. The Bojan goal at Stoke and the Theo Walcott goal for the Gunners are evidence of how vulnerable City have been in that regard.

Jeff Schlupp and Marc Albrighton, plus current right-back incumbent Ritchie De Laet, have the athleticism to play the wing-back roles, while a three-man midfield may be more familiar to Gökhan Inler and N'Golo Kanté.

Inler seems more suited to a holding role, while the security that position would provide would help with Kanté's development because while he is all-action and hunts the ball down like a hungry jackal, he is still learning positionally how to play in the Premier League.

The one drawback would be that Riyad Mahrez would not be able to play in a wide position, where Ranieri believes he is at his best and where he can get into one-on-one situations. The way he has started this season would back up that view.

Ranieri certainly has plenty of options to consider even if he doesn't change system. At left-back he has the choice between Schlupp's pace and power down the flank and, in Austria captain Christian Fuchs, who has been impressive in the Capital One Cup so far, an experienced head who probably provides greater defensive knowledge and security than Schlupp, plus superb delivery from the left, even if he lacks Schlupp's athleticism.

Ranieri has an abundance of options from this squad and that puts greater pressure on him to get his selection right.

Things have gone so well for the Italian so far this season that not many of his decisions can be called into question, although I was extremely surprised that when he, quite rightly, brought on the statuesque figure of Leonardo

Ulloa to boost City's attack last week it was at the expense of Albrighton, who had been providing a wealth of dangerous crosses from the left.

But I suspect he won't depart too far from the system and personnel he has chosen so far and it will be business as usual at Carrow Road, with the Arsenal game regarded as a mere bump in the road.

If it was the first acid test of Ranieri's reign, he passed with flying colours. Controversially, he left out Riyad Mahrez, who had scored five goals and contributed three assists already, and changed both his full-backs as Christian Fuchs and Danny Simpson came into the side. It would be the first appearance of the back four that would form such an effective rearguard as the season progressed.

With Jeff Schlupp now pushed forward on the left wing, City lost none of their counter-attacking intent and took the lead when N'Golo Kanté, who was starting to show he had acclimatised to life in the Premier League, played in Vardy, who drew a challenge from Sébastien Bassong and went down to earn a penalty, which he converted himself to make it six goals in five games. Vardy became the pantomime villain with the Canaries fans, who accused him of diving. It wasn't the first time Vardy had been tarred with that brush. He had won several penalties during City's Championship season and Nigel Pearson had sprung to his defence, saying it was Vardy's ability to commit defenders to challenges they shouldn't be making that was proving so effective. This was a classic example of that trick.

City broke again in the second half for Schlupp to make it 2-0 and again Kanté was at the heart of it, but there was to be no first clean sheet of the season for City as Dieumerci Mbokani grabbed a late consolation for the Canaries.

Incredibly, City were up to fourth in the Premier League table with 15 points after eight games. It had taken them 21 games to reach 17 points the previous campaign. This was already turning out better than many had imagined at the start of the season, and Vardy was starting to garner head-lines with his sensational start to the season. Former City striker Alan Smith said Vardy was tearing up the Premier League with his sensational form and Ranieri said England needed a striker of Jamie Vardy's qualities.

LEICESTER MERCURY BLOG, 14 OCTOBER 2015
JAMIE VARDY ENGLAND STRIKER

The life of a football writer can be quite parasitic.

Especially covering just one club, like Leicester City.

Sometimes it is to the journalist's detriment. But if you are lucky enough to follow the right club then it can be a positive.

The journalist's fortunes and experiences can depend very much on the success of the club they follow, and that certainly has been the case for me following City.

Over the past six years I have been able to follow City abroad, I have been able to work in the Premier League and go to the biggest and best grounds in the country, and recently I have been able to cover England games at Wembley.

That is down simply to the form of Jamie Vardy.

It has been a long time since I have been to Wembley. I thought I was going when City went 3-1 up at Cardiff City in the play-offs, and when Anthony Knockaert won that penalty at Watford, only for those hopes to be dashed on both occasions.

But because of Vardy's inclusion in Roy Hodgson's squad I have been able to cover the Switzerland and Estonia games in recent months, and it has been a pleasure, despite both games being uninspiring in many respects.

It has been a good experience to follow Vardy's emergence, but I couldn't help feeling sorry for him on Monday night in Lithuania.

He has picked up four caps now and no one can take them away from him, but I can't help feeling he hasn't been given the right opportunity by Hodgson to really showcase his strengths.

Vardy has demonstrated, without a shadow of a doubt, that he is at his best when he is played down the middle and given the freedom to use his pace and tenacious running to put defenders under pressure, work the channels and run into space. The shackles have been off and Claudio Ranieri, and City, have benefitted.

It has been very different with England where, by and large, Vardy has been tied to the left-hand side, where his strengths are nullified.

One of Vardy's strengths is his relentless and unpredictable movement in between and in behind defenders, exploiting any space they have disregarded. On the left those opportunities are limited.

Plus, playing in an England side that dominates possession means much of his work has to be done in front of deep-lying defences, whereas he has been most effective for City when he has had space to run in behind defensive lines.

The one time Vardy appeared to be given the opportunity to play his usual game was when he came on as a substitute against Estonia and he immediately forced an error out of a defender with his pressurising and set up a goal for Raheem Sterling. That was the Vardy we see every week, not the guy who struggled to get into the game in Lithuania.

I hope he gets another chance in the upcoming friendlies against Spain, France and Germany because those games may actually suit him more, if he is played in the right position.

This was a long way from his humble beginnings in Sheffield. Vardy's story is one of the most incredible in the modern football era.

As a 16-year-old, Vardy had been released by Sheffield Wednesday, the club he had grown up supporting and for whom he dreamt of playing. He actually gave up football altogether for a while, his dream of becoming a professional seemingly shattered.

'When I was released it was hard to take,' Vardy recalls. 'When you get into an academy and you are playing football every day of the week that is all you ever want to do. When I got released, it was real heartache. The academy director told me I was too small. That was one of the reasons I stopped because I thought I would never be a professional footballer because I had been released. I had supported them all my life and it was a really low blow. It made me think football was not for me and that is why I took the seven months out of the game. Luckily for me my mate got me back into it and I started enjoying it again.'

He then started playing as a youth player for Stocksbridge Park Steels in Sheffield, a Northern Premier League side in the non-league pyramid, progressing from the youth team to the reserves and finally the first team, while working as a carbon fibre technician making aids for people who suffer from drop foot.

'I remember my first wage with Stocksbridge,' Vardy adds. 'I was a youth player and after getting called up to the first team I was paid £30 a week. I had never earned money through football. I was happy to get that. I was working full time at the time so it was tough. There were long hours at work in the day and then playing football at night.

'I got a move to Halifax which was brilliant but the work was taking its toll on me. It was doing my back in so I decided to just quit and live off the football money. We had to do a lot of heavy lifting into ovens and the shelves we had to put items on were way above my height. When you have to do that on a daily basis and you are lifting about 100 times a day it damages your back so it was time to stop. It didn't stop me playing football. If anything it was playing football the night before and then ringing up work the next day and saying I was injured to get off work, to be honest.

'They were long days, I'll tell you that. Before I signed for Fleetwood there was only training two nights of the week – Tuesday and Thursday – then a game Saturday. If I had training, it was up at 7am, in for work, finish work at 4.15–4.30pm, straight in the car to meet up with the other lads from Halifax and we were training and not getting home until 10pm or 11pm. Then straight to bed. That is just how it was, but it was a learning curve. It was a good experience to be honest, especially with how physical it is in non-league. There are tackles that go in which you'd never dream about getting away with nowadays, but that is just how it is.

'It was dinner at work then stop off at the service station before we met up with the lads. The England chefs probably wouldn't approve, but back then it was whichever fast-food shop was at the service station. You needed to get a bit of food down you. It was as simple as that.'

There were other problems to overcome, not just juggling a gruelling, physical job with the demands of non-league football. Vardy was convicted of assault after he defended a deaf friend who was being targeted by a group in a pub and had to wear an ankle tag for six months, and observe a strict curfew between 6pm and 6am.

'I was out one night with a friend who wore a hearing aid and two lads for no reason thought it would be funny to start knocking him and attack him,' Vardy explains. 'I am not proud of what I did but I stuck up for him and defended him, as I would for any mate. It ended up getting me into a bit of trouble. That is one of the things that has made me the person I am.'

'It made the football more difficult. On a few occasions I had to literally leap over the fence and get in the car to get back to avoid breaking my curfew. My mum and dad would pick me up. The away games, if they were too far, I could only play an hour. I would have to come off, hope we were winning and straight back into the car to get home in time.

'It was hard. It had an effect on your family as well because I was in the house constantly. I couldn't leave. It was tough not being able to do what any normal 20-year-old wants to do. I couldn't go out; I was locked in the house. All my mates would be out but I was sat at home.'

After quitting work to concentrate on football with Halifax, he was soon snapped up by Fleetwood Town, who were chasing promotion from the Conference to the Football League and Vardy flourished as a professional. He scored 34 goals as Fleetwood won the Conference title. He also developed his reputation as a prankster as well as a goal-scorer, once performing a streak of the training pitch as a forfeit.

'I can't remember why but it was normally something to do with being late or the worst prank of the day,' Vardy says. 'It was around winter and it was freezing. It is always freezing up in Fleetwood anyway so I wasn't messing about. I did my lap as quick as I could and straight back into the showers. All the lads on the balcony were laughing and giving me the wolf whistles. I literally sprinted it at three-quarter pace all the way around.

'They were good times at Fleetwood. If you had asked me back then I would never have thought I would have signed for Leicester City. I was just at Fleetwood and we were on a mission to get into the Football League. I thought that was where I would be after we got promoted as well. I never thought this would happen.'

City manager Nigel Pearson, who lives in Sheffield, had been aware of Vardy's growing reputation from his days at Stocksbridge and had monitored his progress at Halifax and Fleetwood before deciding to spend £1 million, a record for a player from a non-league club, to bring him to Leicester in 2012. Vardy struggled in that first season and admitted he started to doubt whether he could replicate his non-league form in the Championship.

'The first season after I stepped out of non-league, if I'm honest, was a struggle and I did get doubts in my head, but the manager at the time, Nigel Pearson, had a nice chat with me and told me it was exactly where I belonged,' he said. 'It made me try even harder. In the second season we got promoted and I chipped in with a few goals.

'It was a big jump and that was one of the reasons why I might have struggled to start with, but having that full year training full-time constantly and getting experience meant the second season was where it really kicked on.'

Vardy then played a key role in City's promotion to the Premier League, and he completed his meteoric rise to finally become an England international. Vardy admits the Premier League and Wembley were a long way from his non-league roots.

'I never thought I could make it to the Premier League, I am not going to lie to you,' he admits. 'I just wanted to keep improving as much as I could and see where that got me. That is one of the reasons why I did quit my job. I just wanted to give it a good go that season. Luckily, three days later, I got the move to Fleetwood and that was full-time football anyway.

'There is a lot of hard work that has gone into this, I am not going to lie. I still pinch myself most days before I even got here. You would never have thought from where I have come from this was ever on the cards. I have this opportunity now so I want to go out there and prove I am worthy.'

Vardy has certainly proved he now belongs in the Premier League, and he would continue to dominate the headlines and set records during the season.

Vardy was just getting started.

VARDY BECOMES A CITY LEGEND AND IT'S PIZZA TIME

It seemed nothing could stop City's number 9, not even two broken bones in his right wrist. Vardy had suffered the injury during the comeback win over Aston Villa at the King Power Stadium and had played every game since then wearing a lightweight cast. Vardy had worn a cast before, during the Championship title season, having punched a test-your-strength punching game in a Blackpool arcade a little too ferociously and followed through, striking the back of the game – Vardy doesn't do anything by halves, even arcade games – but this latest injury was picked up in the cause of duty. It hadn't hampered him. In fact his form, and City's remarkable start to the season, just kept getting better and better.

Once again, Claudio Ranieri's men found themselves with a mountain to climb having gone 2-0 behind against Southampton at St Mary's. The Saints looked like giants compared to City. With the exception of Robert Huth and Wes Morgan, City lacked physical stature. Ironically, after Huth and Morgan, City's next best defender of set-pieces was striker Leonardo Ulloa, but he was missing through injury. José Fonte and Virgil van Dijk, a giant of a Dutchman, had put the Saints in command, but it was a position City were familiar with and they didn't panic. At the break Ranieri made a double change, bringing on Riyad Mahrez and former Saints winger Nathan Dyer for Jeff Schlupp, who needed ten stitches in a head wound after a nasty clash of heads with Cédric, and the ineffective Shinji Okazaki.

The changes turned the game around. Dyer teed up Vardy for the first as City laid siege to the Saints goal, but the equaliser didn't come, despite 18 efforts on goal, until the last minute when Mahrez played Vardy through and he smashed an unstoppable shot past Kelvin Davis in the Saints goal. It took Vardy's tally to nine from the first nine games and he was one game away from equalling Arthur Rowley's and Arthur Chandler's City record of scoring in seven consecutive games ahead of the visit of Crystal Palace – although neither of those men achieved their record in the top flight.

The substitutions had played their part, but so had the Blue Army, and Vardy was quick to praise their contribution afterwards. Supporters can be cynical about footballers praising the fans. Do they mean it or are they merely paying lip service? Vardy genuinely meant it as he mentioned the impressive away support without prompting during an interview with me in the Mixed Zone (which was strangely in the concourse under the stand) after the game.

'The Leicester fans are brilliant,' he told me. 'We were 2-0 down today and they never stopped singing. As soon as we got that first goal you could see what was going to happen. We were on top and got the second goal, and the fans have gone barmy. We need the fans behind us and they have done that again.'

The City support had indeed been terrific. Indeed, it had been a feature of the season. The more City found it difficult, the more the Blue Army would roar them on. At Stoke and at home to Aston Villa they had done this and City had turned the game around, and now at Southampton it was exactly the same. Vardy's words were not empty, they were genuine.

The feeling was mutual. Vardy was becoming a particular favourite with the Blue Army. His energetic and fully committed displays struck a chord. As a supporter, that is the very least you expect from the players. Given the opportunity to pull on the club shirt every supporter would do the same, but City fans could identify with Vardy. They could see something of themselves in him. A working-class boy who had got where he was through sheer graft and determination and was now prepared to give everything to make the most of his time at the top. There were times after games when Vardy would literally shuffle like a geriatric old man through the Mixed Zone, so exhausted was he. He picked up knocks and scrapes, but they never seemed to stop him; nothing could stop him.

A week later, against Palace at the King Power Stadium, Vardy equalled the achievement of Rowley and Chandler with the only goal in a 1-0 win to make it seven consecutive games in which he had scored. Vardy became only the eighth player, and the fifth Englishman, to score in seven consecutive Premier League games, joining Thierry Henry, Alan Shearer,

Ian Wright, Ruud van Nistelrooy, Emmanuel Adebayor, Mark Stein and Daniel Sturridge in achieving the feat.

It was a fine finish too, demonstrating the incredible level of self-belief now radiating from Vardy. Mahrez, who had returned to the starting line-up, played Vardy through with another exquisite pass. In the past, in Vardy's first season with City, he would have snatched at the chance, ploughed a shot straight at advancing Palace keeper Wayne Hennessey; but this was a different Vardy, one who could combine his insatiable work ethic with a touch of class. He skilfully lifted the ball over Hennessey, jumped over him and calmly applied the killer touch.

It was also City's first clean sheet of the season. After weeks of promising pizzas and hotdogs to his players if they managed to shut a team out, Ranieri was going to have to pay out. He had joked that perhaps City's inability to keep a clean sheet was because his players didn't like pizza, and at every press conference he was asked something pizza-related. For those who attended every City press conference the joke was starting to wear thin, so it was a relief when it was finally pizza time.

Ranieri took all his players to Leicester restaurant Peter Pizzeria for lunch, but there was a catch: the players had to make their own pizzas. There was great hilarity as the players tossed pizza dough amidst clouds of flour. It was a brilliant piece of team bonding and another example of Ranieri's light-hearted approach.

A much-changed side had gone to Hull City two days before for the Capital One Cup clash against the Championship side and it had ended in a penalty defeat, Mahrez missing the crucial spot-kick. He had himself put City ahead ten minutes into the first half of extra time after a goalless stalemate, only for Abel Hernandez to equalise for the Tigers.

LEICESTER MERCURY BLOG, 27 OCTOBER 2015
RANIERI PLAYS A BLINDER

I have a confession.

When Claudio Ranieri became the new manager of Leicester City I had a sense of trepidation about the appointment.

No matter how Nigel Pearson allowed himself to be perceived publicly, I had seen how the club had grown behind the scenes, how people at Belvoir Drive had responded to him and how unified his squad was.

I was concerned that Ranieri would erode those solid foundations, make wholesale changes and take City in a completely different direction.

I was expecting the revolution that followed the arrival of another genial gentleman and experienced overseas manager, Sven-Göran Eriksson, a few years previously. Too much change in too short a time period.

I wasn't alone. A lot of the Midlands press pack I spoke to had similar concerns, while many supporters were less than enthused.

I was completely wrong.

Since his arrival Ranieri has played a blinder.

He has played the cards he inherited absolutely spot on.

He has identified the good work that has already been done and the quality of the staff he has at his disposal and given them the freedom to carry on.

He has recognised the quality in the squad and the strengths the players possess and nurtured them, instead of looking to make changes.

Take the emergence of Jamie Vardy as a classic example.

Vardy's strength is his tenacious, aggressive and unpredictable running, so Ranieri has given him the freedom to utilise that strength.

As a result Vardy has grown in confidence and while no one could have predicted he would score ten goals in the opening ten games to lead the goalscorers' chart, he has developed into a top Premier League striker.

Danny Drinkwater is another player who has flourished this season after being given extra responsibility in midfield. He has revelled in the role.

Ranieri has adopted an attacking style of play which has brought the best out of his forward-thinking players.

Marc Albrighton is pumping crosses into the box with astonishing frequency, while Jeff Schlupp now looks a lot more effective as a winger rather than a left-back. It is no coincidence. Both have been given freedom.

Then there is Riyad Mahrez, who is currently one of the most effective midfield players in the Premier League.

Mahrez started the season superbly on the right flank but after signs teams were getting to grips with him in that role Ranieri took the surprising decision to leave him out at Norwich City. It worked a treat as City produced a solid away performance and followed that up at Southampton, when Mahrez and Nathan Dyer were introduced at half-time to attack a large, lumbering Saints back four.

On Saturday, Ranieri put Mahrez back in from the start to operate just in behind Vardy and, surprise, surprise, it was Mahrez who sent Vardy away to score the winner with an exquisite pass.

Ranieri is currently in the zone. Everything he has touched so far has turned to gold.

Of course, inevitably there will be times when it will feel like absolutely nothing is going right, but City are currently in a purple patch and the Blue Army is loving it.

And Ranieri is continuing to prove the doubters wrong.

The disappointment of the cup exit was quickly wiped away by Mahrez; he was City's key man in their next game, at The Hawthorns, as the Foxes again came from behind to record their sixth win of the season to move up to third in the table – although Vardy stole his thunder with his 11th goal in 11 league games, taking him to within just two games of equalling Ruud van Nistelrooy's Premier League record of scoring in ten consecutive games.

Against an Albion side that started the game with four centre-backs on the pitch, and two more waiting on the substitutes' bench, City created a host of chances but then went behind from a set-piece. When Albion went in at half-time ahead through Salomón Rondón's goal, City didn't flinch. They had been in that position so many times it was almost the norm, like a boxer who needed to feel a heavy blow before he came back swinging.

City then blew Albion away at the start of the second half. Marc Albrighton swung in a superb cross for Mahrez to equalise at the back post and then repeated the trick seven minutes later. Vardy then combined superbly with Danny Drinkwater before putting the game beyond the Baggies, who grabbed a late consolation through Rickie Lambert's penalty.

The comeback kings had done it again. City finished the month third in the table and just three points behind leaders Manchester City and second-placed Arsenal.

OCTOBER SUMMARY

Competition	Date	Fixture
Premier League	Sat 3 Oct	Norwich 1-2 Leicester
Premier League	Sat 17 Oct	Southampton 2-2 Leicester
Premier League	Sat 24 Oct	Leicester 1-0 Crystal Palace
League Cup – Fourth Round	Tue 27 Oct	Hull 1-1 Leicester (Hull City win 5-4 on penalties)
Premier League	Sat 31 Oct	West Brom 2-3 Leicester

*Three wins and a draw in the league in October
saw odds slashed repeatedly:*

1000-1 – 17 October (after drawing at Southampton)

750-1 – 24 October (after winning at home to Crystal Palace)

500-1 – 31 October (after winning at West Brom)

NOVEMBER 2015

		P	W	D	L	GF	GA	GD	Pts
1	Manchester City	11	8	1	2	26	9	17	25
2	Arsenal	11	8	1	2	21	8	13	25
3	Leicester City	11	6	4	1	23	19	4	22
4	Manchester United	11	6	3	2	15	8	7	21

Standings on 1 November

VARDY MANIA

'There is no better feeling for a striker than scoring, not at the moment. Everything I'm touching's going in. Long may that continue,' said Jamie Vardy.

The stunning form of Leicester City, and in particular Riyad Mahrez and Vardy, was capturing the attention of the watching world. It was as if everyone was suddenly waking up to what City were doing and to the abilities of their match-winning duo. Mahrez's ability to ghost in off the right flank on his favoured left foot and beat defenders with sublime moments of trickery were delighting the watching public. They marvelled at the fact City had unearthed such a gem and had been able to sign him for just £400,000, a ridiculously low amount for a player of such quality. They were also questioning how a player as naturally talented as Mahrez had been able to go under the radar for so long.

However, it was Vardy who was really grabbing all the attention and all the talk ahead of City's clash with Watford was about whether he could chase down Ruud van Nistelrooy's Premier League goalscoring record of hitting the net in ten consecutive games.

Journalists from around the world were entranced by Vardy's rags-to-riches story and everyone wanted to find out more about him. It was Vardy mania as the world's media lapped up his story of rejection and rejuvenation. Inevitably, that drew some negative headlines too as parts of his family life were exposed by a national newspaper, but Vardy didn't let it affect his performances. He was in the form of his life; he had the Midas touch and he was determined to make the most of his moment in the sun. After all the years of toil, this was his reward.

The fact that all the attention was falling so much on just one member of the team may have caused issues in other dressing rooms, where large egos could get bruised, but not within the City camp. 'All the boys want him to get past that mark,' said teammate Danny Drinkwater, referring to Van Nistelrooy's record. 'It'll be a great achievement for him and it'll look great on the team for helping get there.'

Goalkeeper Kasper Schmeichel questioned whether there was any striker better than Vardy in the league. 'For me he is the best striker in the Premier League right now,' he said. 'You could see from the first training session that he had something about him. He had a tough spell the first six months as he adjusted to the Championship from non-league because it is a big step up, but then he gained his confidence and he hasn't looked back.

'He drags us through and sets the tone every single game. When you have a player like that, he is a dream to play with. You hit balls and clearances and he makes something of them. He turns them into good balls because he chases everything down and never gives up. He is a delight to play with.'

The other consequence of the attention was the speculation that other clubs were plotting to try and steal City's dynamic duo away during the forthcoming transfer window. A day hardly passed without a report somewhere linking either Vardy or Mahrez with some of the biggest names in the game.

Mahrez was being linked with Manchester United, with some reports even suggesting United had already contacted his representatives to gauge if he would be interested in the move – reports that would turn out to be false.

'That is good, because that means we have very good players,' said Ranieri of the mounting speculation. 'It's good.

One week it's Vardy, the next week it's Riyad, another week I don't know who, but this is only speculation. Riyad is happy with us; he renewed his contract [in the summer of 2015]. We want to grow up and then he will stay with us, as well as Jamie Vardy.'

The calls for England boss Roy Hodgson to give Vardy a chance in the role he was proving so effective in for City appeared to irritate the England boss in the week before the Watford clash. 'When you have only played two games you are in no position to go to the coach and say: "I will play for England but only in this position." That is the point I am trying to make,' said Hodgson as he announced his latest squad.

Vardy had never made any such demands, but he was presenting a cast-iron case for him to have a more prominent role for his country with every game and every goal, and he was City's match-winner again against the Hornets. N'Golo Kanté put City ahead with his first goal for the club in the second half, although he was helped by some horrendous goalkeeping by Heurelho Gomes, who let the diminutive Frenchman's toe-poke slip through his grasp. Then there was the familiar sight of Vardy chasing down Wes Morgan's pass into space behind the Watford defence and drawing the foul from Gomes, resulting in a spot-kick which Vardy took and smashed straight down the middle to move to within one game of Van Nistelrooy. Mahrez was actually the designated penalty taker but he demonstrated his generosity and the determination of Vardy's teammates to help him chase down the record by handing the ball to the number 9. Troy Deeney, who inflicted so much pain on City in that fateful play-off second leg at Vicarage Road in 2013, pulled a goal back from the penalty spot but there was to be no late drama on this occasion and City marched onwards.

Not surprisingly, Vardy was named the Premier League

player of the month for October, only the third City player in the history of the Premier League to receive the accolade – Muzzy Izzet and Tim Flowers being the other two – but Vardy wasn't finished. He was full of confidence.

City's assistant manager and head of recruitment, Steve Walsh, the man who had scouted Vardy, revealed he and Nigel Pearson had been watching Vardy for a considerable time, even back to his Stocksbridge Park Steels days.

'We had him tracked from the early stages when he had been released by Sheffield Wednesday and I think he didn't play football for round about three years, and then he joined Stocksbridge Park Steels,' Walsh said. 'We had one or two contacts in that region who watched him play and they said he wasn't bad. It is obviously a massive jump from that level to where we were at the time, but he moved on to Halifax Town. Again we had him watched and were still very impressed with his progress. He had got better obviously playing at the next standard.

'Then he moved on to Fleetwood Town in the Conference. At that stage it gets a little bit more serious but he did particularly well in those games. I was then attracted to it and watched Jamie myself live. We were actually at Hull City at the time. I kept it to myself and then consequently we joined Leicester and we decided he was a striker we could take a punt on. We didn't expect to end up paying the kind of money we ended up paying, I have to say. I probably saw him three or four times in total. I remember talking to Micky Mellon at the time, who was the manager of Fleetwood, and he knew he was going to lose the player. He said he could be anything he wants to be. It came to fruition, although it was a big call to pay £1 million for him.'

That call was now paying off in spades. Vardy was the in-form striker in the Premier League and everyone was willing him to equal Van Nistelrooy's record at St James's Park against Newcastle United.

'It is unbelievable,' said midfielder Andy King. 'You look at the names he has already surpassed to get to second in that list and it is brilliant. You can see everyone around him, the whole city and the team is behind him.'

Even Van Nistelrooy was urging Vardy on to equal his record, tweeting a good luck message to Vardy: '#Records are there to be broken. Go on @vardy7, all the best and good luck!'

Vardy had missed England's friendly against France, which became a poignant occasion following the terrorist attacks in Paris, in which 130 people died in a series of shootings and bomb blasts, because of a hip problem he had picked up during the win over Watford, and was a doubt for the trip to Tyneside.

The Premier League confirmed that even if he did miss a game, as long he scored on his next appearance the record would still be valid, but Vardy, who had spent most of the week in a cryogenic chamber, enduring temperatures of minus 120°C in a bid to be fit, was declared ready and all eyes were on him as he strode out at St James's Park. He didn't let them down. The sub-zero temperatures helped him maintain his red-hot form.

The 3,200 members of the Blue Army, who looked down from their eagle's nest position at the top of Newcastle's giant stand, watched on as not only did Jamie Vardy score the goal that ensured he equalled Van Nistelrooy's Premier League record – at the same time equalling Tony Cottee's record of 13 Premier League goals in a season for City, incredibly after just 13 games – they also saw City win at St James's Park for the first time in 15 years and record their fourth consecutive league win to go top of the Premier League. It was their best ever start to a Premier League season. City also extended another club record as well, for the longest unbeaten Premier League away run, stretching back ten games to March.

In first half added time, Vardy combined superbly with Leonardo Ulloa and then cut past a static Newcastle defence before firing past Rob Elliot. The entire City side raced to celebrate with Vardy while the away section in the upper tier of the stand rejoiced.

It got even better. Leonardo Ulloa was teed up by Mahrez for the second and then Shinji Okazaki completed a comprehensive victory with another scruffy, trademark goal. At the final whistle, the City players pushed Vardy forward to receive the adulation of their supporters, and the Newcastle fans also acknowledged his feat as he walked off the pitch.

'It is a brilliant feeling but the main thing is coming away with the three points,' Vardy said as he stood on the side of the pitch, with the chilly north-east wind bellowing around the now empty and cavernous St James's Park.

'You try to put it in the back of your mind and get on with it. At the end of the day it is a game of football we needed to win. We have done that and I have managed to get my goal as well, so happy days.

'I was very close [to missing the game], I am not going to lie. It is credit to the physios, especially Dave Rennie, who have been working on me constantly. I have been in that cryo chamber and it is absolutely freezing, but it helps in your recovery so fair play to the club for getting that in. This weather feels like I am still in it. It was freezing.'

Having equalled the record, Vardy had the opportunity to break it, ironically against Manchester United, Van Nistelrooy's former club, at the King Power Stadium. The focus in the build-up was all on Vardy. There was hardly a television programme or radio show that wasn't discussing his incredible form, while media representatives from all over the world were calling me to talk about him.

LEICESTER MERCURY BLOG, 25 NOVEMBER 2015
A MEDIA SENSATION

It feels as though the world has suddenly realised that Leicester City exist.

Over the past few weeks, as City have embarked on this extraordinary run of form, the profile of the club has increased, but the drip, drip of media coverage from outside Leicestershire has now become a torrent since they went top of the table last week.

City, and in particular Jamie Vardy, are being discussed on every radio station, in every national newspaper and it seems like Sky Sports News has become LCFC TV.

You can't turn the channel on without them asking whoever what they think of City and Vardy. Today it was Didier Drogba and former City boss Peter Taylor, the last man to lead a City side to the top of the Premier League 15 years ago.

But it isn't just within these shores. There have been requests coming into Mercury Towers from overseas newspapers and television companies asking for information, comment and interviews on City's emergence.

Tomorrow a Danish television company are coming in to film me talking about City, while a French crew asked for local information for their production.

It hasn't been surprising how little was actually known about City, but that is all about to change for both the club and the players, especially Vardy.

The dark side of all the attention is the intrusion. City

have been able to operate within a bubble for the past few years, especially under Nigel Pearson.

That bubble has now burst.

Vardy has already experienced the intrusion into his private life, a nasty by-product of the adulation.

The problem with being an unknown is that when the media start to notice you they want to know more about you, including the skeletons in the closet.

The other side of the coin is the praise that is being heaped upon City, Claudio Ranieri and the players.

Ranieri is far too long in the tooth to take any notice of the adulation as he knows from experience that this week's fans are next week's critics.

The danger is the players who have never experienced this before. Will they believe the hype? Will they become hypnotised by the words of flattery? Will they allow themselves to be washed along on a tide of tribute?

I don't think that will happen as the players I have interviewed have always seemed pretty level-headed and down to earth, especially Vardy.

Besides, there are enough leaders and dressing-room enforcers who won't allow that to happen. If one of the players starts to look as though they are getting a bit too big for their boots there are players within the camp who will police that.

One character who gives that impression is Andy King. Mild-mannered, rational and intelligent, King has emerged as one of the most influential characters within the City camp, along with captain Wes Morgan and vice-captain Kasper Schmeichel.

They will make sure that the players see all the media attention for what it is: a mere sideshow to the main event.

Everyone was willing Vardy to go on to break Van Nistelrooy's record, even Van Nistelrooy. 'I sent him a message of support last weekend on social media and I really meant it,' said the Dutchman in an interview with the *Daily Mail.* 'It would be fantastic for him. I really mean it: records are there to be broken. He can score one on Saturday, in fact I hope he does but hopefully United score three and win 3-1. But no, seriously, if he does it, I'll be delighted for him.'

It isn't often that Manchester United are left in the shadows, but that was the case when they arrived at the King Power Stadium for the late Saturday kick-off. Even the fact that it was a clash between the two top sides in the division, a David-and-Goliath contest between the upstarts from the East Midlands and the established Premier League giants seemed to be a sub-plot to Vardy and Van Nistelrooy's record.

Again, Vardy had spent the week undergoing the cryo chamber treatment and Ranieri admitted in the build-up to the game that he wasn't 100 per cent physically fit, but he was raring to go mentally.

The City fans and the watching world didn't have to wait long; just 24 minutes to be precise. Typically, it came after City turned defence into attack within seconds and when Christian Fuchs clipped in a delightful pass behind the United defence, there seemed to be only one outcome. After beating David De Gea with an instinctive finish Vardy raced away, the euphoria etched on his face, like a modern Marco Tardelli, pointing to his chest and screaming: 'It's mine, all mine.'

Bastian Schweinsteiger ensured it was honours even but the result seemed almost irrelevant. All the talk after the game was about Vardy and that record.

'He thoroughly deserves all the plaudits he is getting at the moment,' said teammate Danny Drinkwater. 'Long may it continue. He is always wanting to better himself and I guess that is the key to his success. His work rate is phenomenal and he is getting his rewards now.'

'Before the game I said to the players we had two aims, to win the match and try to help Jamie break the record,' said Ranieri. 'We drew the match and I am very glad, but I am very proud of the record for Jamie. It is outstanding. He is a great player, a great champion, a great man. It is very important for us.'

The man himself looked drained as he shuffled into the Mixed Zone to speak after the game. It wasn't just physical fatigue after putting in his usual incredible effort; the hype and the pressure in the build-up to the game must have been equally debilitating.

'I couldn't let it get to me, it is as simple as that,' he said. 'If I let it get to me then it goes into the team's performance and it means the lads will be playing with a man down. As soon as I step over the white line I had to make sure that is in the back of my mind and I concentrate on my game. Luckily that is what I have done and I have managed to get on the end of Christian Fuchs's pass and slotted it home.'

Throughout the streak the City fans had been singing 'Jamie Vardy is having a party'. Now it was time to let the party commence.

NOVEMBER SUMMARY

Competition	Date	Fixture
Premier League	Sat 7 Nov	Leicester 2-1 Watford
Premier League	Sat 21 Nov	Newcastle 0-3 Leicester
Premier League	Sat 28 Nov	Leicester 1-1 Man Utd

*An unbeaten November saw Leicester move joint top of
the Premier League as the odds continued to shorten:*

200-1 – 7 November (after winning at home to Watford)

100-1 – 22 November (the day after winning at Newcastle)

50-1 – 28 November (after drawing at home with Manchester United)

DECEMBER 2015

		P	W	D	L	GF	GA	GD	Pts
1	Manchester City	14	9	2	3	30	14	16	29
2	Leicester City	14	8	5	1	29	21	8	29
3	Manchester United	14	8	4	2	20	10	10	28
4	Arsenal	14	8	3	3	24	12	12	27

Standings on 1 December

MAHREZ, MONK AND MOURINHO

City were now level on points with Manchester City at the top of the Premier League. It was unfamiliar territory for the club and Ranieri's men were now being compared to the great City sides of the past.

In 1928/29 City finished second in the old first division, missing out on the championship by one point. It was the highest position the club had ever achieved. They won the last game of the season 6-1 but Sheffield Wednesday took the title.

The 1963 team were known as the Ice Kings for their ability to mount a title challenge through the worst winter the country had experienced in 200 years. The conditions were so severe that many clubs were unable to play. The FA Cup third round that season took 66 days to complete and there were a total of 261 postponements during the season.

City had won ten games on the trot, seven in the league and three in the cup, and very nearly won the league and cup double that season. When they beat Bill Shankly's Liverpool in the FA Cup semi-final, they were second in the table. They were playing Manchester United, who were fighting relegation, in the FA Cup final and people genuinely thought they had a great chance of winning the double, but unfortunately they picked up several injuries, lost the last four league games and then didn't turn up at Wembley, losing 3-1. It was their second cup final defeat in three years. 'We had a fantastic run from November through to March and had put ourselves in a great position,' recalls former City winger Mike Stringfellow. 'We had a terrible winter which shut down a lot of the country but we were able to keep on playing, which helped us because the other teams had to play catch up. We had also switched to a back four and we were the first team to do so. We didn't concede many goals. I remember when we beat Liverpool in the FA Cup semi-final [Stringfellow scored the only goal] and Bill Shankly called it a travesty and complained about our tactics, but Liverpool were using the same tactics the next season. I don't know why we faded so badly in the last few games. We just didn't become the same side after that win.'

The 1970 Jimmy Bloomfield side were known as the Entertainers, but the nearest they came to winning any-thing was in 1974 when they lost in the FA Cup semi-final to Liverpool.

The most recent period of success for City had been the Martin O'Neill era, when City won two League Cups, in 1997 and 2000, and finished in the top ten for four consecutive seasons between 1997 and 2000.

A downward spiral had ensued but now the good times had returned. City were feeding once again at the top table of English football, even if the established elite were more than a little uncomfortable at the unfashionable urchins from the East Midlands trying to gatecrash their party.

Everyone was still talking about Jamie Vardy after his record-breaking run of scoring in 11 consecutive Premier League games as City prepared to head to South Wales to face Swansea City at the Liberty Stadium.

As well as holding the Premier League record outright, Vardy was also now level with the great Stan Mortensen of Blackpool, who scored in 11 consecutive games in the 1950/51 season, and one away from equalling Irishman Jimmy Dunne's English football league record of scoring in 12 consecutive games, achieved during the 1931/32 season while playing for Sheffield United.

'My friend in Italy asked me about Vardy,' Ranieri said in the build-up to the Swansea game. 'To explain I said I believe

Shinji Okazaki reacts first to acrobatically steer home
his first goal for the club.

West Ham United 1-2 Leicester City • 15 August 2015 • The Boleyn Ground, London

Summer signing Nathan Dyer bravely heads an 89th-minute winner past
Aston Villa's Brad Guzan.

Leicester City 3-2 Aston Villa • 13 September 2015 • The King Power Stadium, Leicester

Jamie Vardy scores in his tenth successive match
to equal the Premier League record …

Newcastle United 0-3 Leicester City • 21 November 2015 • St James' Park, Newcastle

… and then extends the record to 11 with this first-half opener
against Manchester United.

Leicester City 1-1 Manchester United • 28 November 2015 • The King Power Stadium, Leicester

© Neil Plumb/Plumb Images

Goals from Mahrez and Vardy were enough to see off Chelsea and would mean
the end of Mourinho's second spell as manager.

Leicester City 2-1 Chelsea • 14 December 2015 • The King Power Stadium, Leicester

Robert Huth is mobbed after scoring a late winner
at White Hart Lane to send the Foxes joint top.

Tottenham 0-1 Leicester City • 13 January 2016 • White Hart Lane, London

© Neil Plumb/Plumb Images

**Mahrez celebrates as Leicester confidently sweep aside title rivals Man City
to move five points clear.**

Manchester City 1-3 Leicester City • 6 February 2016 • Etihad Stadium, Manchester

Danny Simpson is sent off against Arsenal as Leicester fall
to their first league defeat of 2016.

Arsenal 2-1 Leicester City • 14 February 2016 • Emirates Stadium, London

Leo Ulloa prods home late on against Norwich,
the only goal in a tough test for the league leaders.

Leicester City 1-0 Norwich • 27 February 2016 • The King Power Stadium, Leicester

© Neil Plumb/Plumb Images

Victory away at Sunderland moves Claudio Ranieri's men
to within three wins of the title.

Sunderland 0-2 Leicester City • 10 April 2016 • The Stadium of Light, Sunderland

Wes Morgan heads Leicester level at Old Trafford
knowing that a win would see them crowned champions.

Manchester United 1-1 Leicester City • 1 May 2016 • Old Trafford, Manchester

The match ends 1-1 and all eyes turn towards Tottenham's game
at Chelsea the following night.

Manchester United 1-1 Leicester City • 1 May 2016 • Old Trafford, Manchester

Leicester City are crowned Premier League champions.

Leicester City 3-1 Everton • 7 May 2016 • The King Power Stadium, Leicester

Club captain Wes Morgan becomes a Premier League champion
for the first time, aged 32.

Leicester City 3-1 Everton • 7 May 2016 • The King Power Stadium, Leicester

Andy King (left), Danny Drinkwater (centre) and Matty James (right)
were all regulars in the Leicester side that won promotion
to the Premier League in 2013/14.

Leicester City 3-1 Everton • 7 May 2016 • The King Power Stadium, Leicester

Claudio Ranieri celebrates with goalkeeper Kasper Schmeichel.

Leicester City 3-1 Everton • 7 May 2016 • The King Power Stadium, Leicester

if Vardy grabs a light bulb, the bulb will switch on – he is electric. Jamie is electric. It is good energy – I should bring him into my house so I don't pay the electricity!'

For once, it would be another City player who would grab the headlines. Vardy had now scored 14 goals in total but Riyad Mahrez's perfect hat-trick at the Liberty Stadium would take his tally to ten in the Premier League and 11 in all competitions to see City move two points clear at the top of the table.

While Vardy is all about determination, pace, power and sheer belligerence, Mahrez is an artistic player. Nothing he does is scruffy or ugly. His first came with a header from a fifth-minute corner, his second with a curling left-foot finish and his third with his right foot in the second half to complete the perfect treble, and that summed up City's aesthetic display. He was the first City player since Stan Collymore in 2000 to score a top-flight hat-trick.

Swansea had hit the woodwork on two occasions but similarly Vardy had chances to equal Dunne's record and inflict an even more emphatic win over the Welshmen. They had been embarrassed on their own patch and had now won only one game in their last 11. Swans boss Garry Monk may have seen his eventual sacking coming and four days later he was relieved of his duties.

He would soon be joined in the managerial dole queue by Chelsea boss José Mourinho – and again it would be City who would apply the final nail in the coffin.

The champions were mounting the worst defence of a Premier League title in the history of the competition and were languishing in 16th place in the table, one point above the relegation zone. Chelsea had scored a combined total of just 17 goals. City duo Vardy and Mahrez alone had scored 24 between them.

Chelsea had been the champions-in-waiting when they had last visited the King Power Stadium, while City had been the side fighting desperately against relegation. The roles were remarkably reversed as Chelsea arrived for City's last home game before hitting the road over Christmas. The table had been turned upside down. Still, not many people were looking at City as possible successors to Chelsea as champions. Riyad Mahrez himself echoed the views of many when he said City would not win the title.

'No, we will not be champions,' said Mahrez. 'We do not have broad enough shoulders. The other teams have bigger squads. At some point, they will overtake us. The title? We are trying to pick up points here and there. We are first but it means nothing. The big teams will all wake up at some point. We are just trying to finish in the best place possible and we will see how it goes.'

Sir Alex Ferguson was one of the few voices making a case for City's candidacy, stating he felt they could kick on in the second half of the season and push for the title if they recruited well in January. The fact that Ferguson, who knew a thing or two about winning the Premier League, having done it 13 times, had backed City made a few people raise their eyebrows.

City were certainly going into the Chelsea game with their tails up. Their fantastic form in November had led to Claudio Ranieri and striker Jamie Vardy being named as the Premier League manager and player of the month. Having been nominated three times it was finally recognition for Ranieri, while Vardy was winning the award for the second consecutive month.

⚽

LEICESTER MERCURY BLOG, 10 DECEMBER 2015
NO FLUKE

It looks as though Leicester City are finally getting all the plaudits they deserve for their incredible start to the season.

Pundits who have been waiting for City's bubble to burst are now accepting that this is actually a very good City side.

They can see that, after 15 games, it is no fluke, and when you include the last nine games of last season as well it is sustained form over 24 games. In that time City have been beaten just twice and have picked up 54 points.

This is now one of the most interesting Premier League seasons for years simply because of the form of clubs like City, Crystal Palace and West Ham United.

Some may say it is a Premier League that lacks quality simply because the big clubs are not as strong as they once were, and they are right when they point out that Manchester United, Manchester City, Chelsea etc. are not that good at the moment.

But take nothing away from the rest of the clubs, especially City, who are showing that it doesn't take millions in the bank to produce an effective, winning team, one that can play a vibrant, attacking brand of football that gets people out of their seats.

City have spent money, of course. They spent over £25 million in the summer, but compared to the likes of Manchester City that is small beer and one look at the City line-up, which has hardly changed all season, reveals the expertise that has gone into putting this squad together.

City are top of the league by right. They deserve to be there at this moment in time.

Now the really hard part begins – staying there.

There have been unfancied sides before who have challenged for the title only to eventually come up short, most memorably Aston Villa in 1989/90 and Norwich City in 1992/93, who were unable to get across the finishing line.

The pressure will start to mount as the season goes on and while City may still be stating that their only goal is to reach 40 points, they must be starting to think about what they could actually achieve this season.

Since the Premier League was formed in 1992, there hasn't been a club to drop out of the top four when they've had this many points after just 15 games. That stat alone will bring increased pressure.

Vardy was everywhere, and not just on the pitch. For the Chelsea match, every seat had a noise clapper placed on it with a message of thanks from Vardy to the fans written on it, while bags of 'Vardy Salted' Walkers crisps were handed out before the game. It was no surprise when it was Vardy who popped up with the opening goal after 34 minutes. It also felt inevitable that it would be Mahrez who would provide the pinpoint pass for the number 9 to score.

The Chelsea starting line-up had cost over £200 million more than City's but their big-name players were overshadowed again by Mahrez, who produced a wonderful curling finish to put City further ahead, and despite a late Loïc Rémy goal, the champions were beaten.

Immediately after the game Mourinho gave a television interview which was startling, not just because he branded the City ball boys a disgrace to the Premier League, but because he said he felt his work in preparing his side for the threats of Vardy and Mahrez had been 'betrayed'. It was seen as an indication of a growing divide between Mourinho and his players.

'All last season I did some phenomenal work and took them to a level that was not their level,' he said. 'It was more than they really are. All this season we are doing so bad. Clearly for some of them it is so difficult.'

Hazard had limped off early in the first half and Mourinho seemed bewildered as to why. 'I don't know [what his injury was]. All I know was within ten seconds he had made the decision himself. It must be a serious injury because he just left the pitch.'

A few days later I was sitting with Ranieri in his spacious office, where he had entertained Mourinho after the game, when the news broke that Mourinho had been sacked by Roman Abramovich for a second time.

Ranieri knows what that feels like.

LEICESTER MERCURY BLOG, 16 DECEMBER 2015
A BREATH OF FRESH AIR

Just when you think it can't get any better, it does!

Leicester City fans must be pinching themselves to believe that City are top of the Premier League going into the Christmas period having just beaten the reigning champions.

It may seem unbelievable considering where they were in March and there are many within the media who simply don't believe it.

Every week they state that this is the week that City's bubble bursts and normal service is resumed.

But every week City seem to defy the odds and continue this extraordinary story.

And how refreshing it is, not just to City supporters but to all football fans who have grown sick of the predictable nature of the Premier League.

For years now we have gone into seasons knowing that either Manchester United, Chelsea, Arsenal (in previous years) and Manchester City (more recently) will contest the title.

There have been some exciting moments, like when Manchester City won their first title in one of the most dramatic finishes to any season ever.

But by and large it has become tedious.

Younger readers, take my word for it, it never used to be so cut and dried.

In the 1980s Liverpool dominated but the likes of Aston Villa, Norwich City, Ipswich Town, Southampton, West Bromwich Albion and Watford were challengers.

Manchester's United and City were not.

And of course Nottingham Forest won the title and two European Cups.

The flood of money that has come into the game since the formation of the Premier League has resulted in the playing field becoming uneven, not just because of the money from television but because the globalisation of the game has attracted billionaires willing to pump even more money into clubs, resulting in a gulf between the have-a-lots and the just haves.

City may have a billionaire owner but compared to Manchester City, Chelsea etc., the club is still miles behind on a spreadsheet.

But not, as they have shown, on the pitch because City have demonstrated that money, no matter how much you spend, is only one part of developing a good club.

This side has been put together over the past three years

and, yes, compared to most Championship clubs City have been able to invest.

But a large portion of that investment has gone into the club's infrastructure: the training ground, the stadium and the backroom staff.

Now, we don't know exactly how much City have spent as all deals are undisclosed but even with the reported fees the side that started on Monday night was put together at very little cost in modern Premier League terms.

Kasper Schmeichel (£1.2 million), Danny Simpson (unknown but under £1 million), Robert Huth (£3 million), Wes Morgan (£1 million), Christian Fuchs (free), Riyad Mahrez (£400,000), Danny Drinkwater (£1 million), N'Golo Kanté (£5.6 million), Marc Albrighton (free), Leonardo Ulloa (£8 million), Jamie Vardy (£1 million).

I was never good at maths but by my reckoning that team was put together for just over £22 million, if we round Simpson's fee up to £1 million.

Compare that to how much Chelsea paid for Diego Costa – and how poor was he on Monday, by the way? Chelsea paid £32 million for Costa. The same as they paid for Eden Hazard. That £22 million combined cost of the City XI is still less than Chelsea paid for Oscar, £25 million.

In fact, a stat that was flying around the press bench on Monday night was that the Chelsea team cost a whopping £200 million more than City's.

City are demonstrating that there is more to the Premier League than money. There are more ingredients required, like commitment, desire, team spirit, good coaching, excellent scouting and recruitment.

Leicester City are, quite simply, a breath of fresh air.

CLAUDIO RANIERI – THE LIKEABLE
ROMAN CONQUEROR

Leicester was conquered by the Romans. Ancient Roman baths and pavements still exist in the city and one of the roads that leads down to the King Power Stadium is named Raw Dykes Road, after the remains of a Roman aqueduct on the hill above the stadium.

The Romans called Leicester *Ratae* but after the Roman withdrawal from Britain the city was eventually conquered by the Danes, and was named in the Domesday Book as *Ledecestre*. Now there was a Roman hand gripping the city again – that of Claudio Ranieri. But this time he wasn't seen as a foreign invader, he was being hailed as a conquering hero. There may have been some trepidation when his appointment was first announced, but Ranieri would soon have the doubters converted and the City fans singing his name. Now they were calling him 'the Godfather'.

The one thing that stands out about Ranieri is that he has the endearing quality of being able to laugh at himself. 'When I was with Chelsea I was known as the Tinkerman,' he said before City's pre-Christmas trip to Everton. 'Now I don't want to change my team. I am waiting for when people change my nickname from Tinkerman to Thinkerman.'

It has probably stood him in good stead in the past because there were times when he was the object of ridicule. His limited English during his time at Chelsea led to him being dubbed 'Clownio', but now, with City, he was demonstrating what everyone in Italy knew: that he was a talented and experienced coach and man-manager.

Unlike many top managers, Ranieri appears to be free of ego. Some managers are belligerent in their insistence that their way is the only way. Not Ranieri. The Italian was showing he had learned from his experiences at Stamford Bridge. Now he had another chance in the Premier League and he seemed determined to take it.

His captain at Chelsea, Marcel Desailly, speaks highly of him but has said that while in charge at Stamford Bridge he ruled with an iron rod and many players were scared of him.

'Ranieri is an experienced coach who knows what he is talking about,' said Desailly. 'He is a leader, sometimes too much to the point where he scares players, but this time [at Leicester] it looks like his communication with the players has been very good.

'He is low profile, very cool and relaxed, but as a coach he is tough. If you try and come in his office and discuss things with him and you are not happy about something, he will push you, he will crush you and you will come out and instead of thinking you have gained something you are suddenly completely down and wonder what is going on.'

It seems Ranieri has mellowed from those days. These days the iron fist is covered by a velvet glove.

City captain Wes Morgan is the man all the players turn to when they need something raised with Ranieri. It is Morgan's job to knock on the manager's door and raise any concerns or fears, but he says he has always found Ranieri's door open.

'I am always knocking on the manager's door and coming into his room and he is like "Wes, what do you want now?" "I just need two minutes" and explain what the boys want,' says Morgan. 'From his point of view, if he has something to tell the boys, he sometimes tells the group or passes it through me first. It is a very good relationship.

'There is that fine line of how far to push him and he has made us know who is boss when it is time to be the boss but at the same time you can have a laugh with him and know how far to push him as well.

'He is quite funny, I am sure you see it in the interviews; he has a few one-liners; the relationship between him and Vards [Vardy] is the best and there is a lot of swearing involved so I can't say too much. They both give as good as they get.'

Ranieri has certainly shown his sense of humour in press conferences with a catalogue of one-liners, humorous quips and his catchphrase 'slowly, slowly'.

If he isn't expressing his admiration for Leicester rock band Kasabian, his love of romantic movies like *Ghost*, or trying to bribe his players with pizza and hot dogs, he is comparing his strikers to the RAF and the Road Runner, complete with 'meep, meep' sound effects. He described N'Golo Kanté and Danny Drinkwater as his bus drivers. He has quoted Kipling (he first read the famous poem 'If' growing up in Rome and fell in love with it), Shakespeare and Barack Obama, and when he revealed he attracts the attention of his players by ringing an imaginary bell, shouting 'dilly-ding, dilly-dong' it was on every television, radio and written press report. Jamie Vardy would later tell us that the players would walk around the training ground and greet each other with a 'dilly-ding, dilly-dong', and for Christmas Ranieri bought them all a real bell. The fans would also adopt it as a terrace anthem.

The comic touch would prove so valuable during the latter part of the season when City were chasing the title. Ahead of the game at Watford, the players knew how important the game was, especially as rivals Tottenham Hotspur and Arsenal had just drawn, giving them a great opportunity to strengthen their position at the top of the table. Vardy has described how there were nerves and tension on the coach to

Vicarage Road – until Jeff Stelling of Sky Sports' *Gillette Soccer Saturday* appeared on the television and did an impression of Ranieri: 'dilly-ding, dilly-dong'. The whole coach burst out laughing and any tension cleared.

If Ranieri knows how to play the press, he immediately showed his gift for man-management when he met up with the squad in Austria just after his appointment. Ranieri did not take an active part in the sessions, instead watching from the sidelines, but when he spoke to the players for the first time it left an impression, so Marc Albrighton says.

'When he first came in at the start of the season, his words were, "I don't think you believe how good this group of players are, if you get that belief in yourself, you will go further as a group." So we are starting to believe that ourselves, so if we can believe it fully like he says then maybe he's right.'

He made good players better by making them believe in themselves even more and aspire to greater accomplishments. This was to be a distinct feature of City's incredible season.

Throughout the campaign the most asked question was: 'How is this possible?' The answer is simply because the players believed it was possible, and that came, from the very start, from Ranieri. Not that he would ever reveal such ambition publicly. His mantra at the start was that the goal was simply to reach 40 points to achieve survival: '40 points, 40 points, then we will see.'

Ranieri is all about respect. He has respect for the Leicester public, whom he meets regularly in the course of his walks around the city, as he frequents his favourite local restaurants with his wife, Rosanna, stopping for photos and autographs willingly. He has respect for his players as men, trusting them to conduct themselves professionally and even giving them a whole week off after the defeat to Arsenal in February; and he has respect for the media.

Above all, his respect for his fellow managers was evident when I was invited into his office at the King Power Stadium just before the Christmas trips to Everton and Liverpool. The large room was sparsely decorated the last time I was invited into the manager's inner sanctum, by Nigel Pearson.

All that remained from Pearson's time was a small drinks fridge. The black leather sofas had changed and were positioned so they faced each other, like a household living room, not an airport waiting lounge as they had been before; the walls had been decorated and a large television hung from one wall, enhancing the homely feel. As I walked in, Football Gold was showing a Chelsea game from Ranieri's era.

On one wall were framed photos of all the Premier League managers. Ranieri said it was to make them feel at home when they visit, but it is also a mark of respect to his peers. Of course, several of those pictures had changed since the start of the season, as Dick Advocaat, Brendan Rodgers and Tim Sherwood had left their positions; Garry Monk's photo still remained on the wall at that point, despite his sacking just days before.

It was during this meeting that the news broke of José Mourinho's sacking by Chelsea – a reminder that the life of a football manager is a precarious one, as Ranieri himself has experienced many times in his career.

Before Leicester, he had managed 13 clubs (including two spells with Valencia) in Italy, Spain and England, and had been sacked on several occasions, most notably at Chelsea where he had shown considerable dignity as he carried on despite Roman Abramovich's rather public push to find his replacement. Ranieri knew he was a dead man walking at Stamford Bridge and often joked that he knew the Sword of Damocles was hanging above his head. But he bore no bitterness.

'Yes, immediately I knew,' he recalls of the end of his Chelsea reign. 'The chief executive [Trevor Birch] told me there is a new owner and I said "Me and you are the first who go home". You imagine, the new owner arrives and he wants to put in his own men. It is normal. If the new owner wants to change something, it is normal. I wanted to show our best and we bought some good players. I wanted to win something.'

At Valencia and at Chelsea there was a sense that Ranieri had laid the foundations for success before the owners parachuted someone else in to finish his good work, but his experiences with the Greek national team were more damaging to his reputation.

'It is not easy to link 11 or even 22 players into a team if you don't have time,' he said of his sacking after just four games, in which Greece lost every match including a humiliating defeat to the Faroe Islands. 'I made a mistake when I was manager of Greece. I wanted to look because it was different between the job at a club and a national team. It was my mistake because it is not my job, it is another job.

'I had four matches and for each game I trained the players for just three days. That is 12 days of training. What can I do in just 12 days? I had to rebuild a national team in just 12 days. What could I do? I am not a magician.'

Greece, the former European champions, were in a mess before Ranieri and after him. In fact they lost again in the Faroe Islands seven months after his departure and have won just two internationals since. But, like so many of his players, Ranieri now had something to prove and the disappointment and rejection had created a hunger in him to restore his reputation once again. He was one of the 'Misfits'. He was also now much more at home amidst the day-to-day bustle of a club on the rise.

Describing his Leicester experience, he said: 'It has been unbelievable. I am an honest man when I say I never expected this. I never thought we could do this and that. When I came here, I thought we must work and I must understand my players, and if they understand my philosophy then we can do something good. Slowly I discover this fantastic group.

'Others told me they were a good group but I have discovered this group is so fantastic. There is a fantastic electricity with the owner, the players, me and all the staff. It is true that everyone is a big family here at Leicester and everyone is working hard to do the best for the team.'

All the while, as we were talking, the news kept coming regarding Roman Abramovich's axing of Mourinho, the man who replaced Ranieri at Chelsea in 2004. Abramovich didn't believe in Ranieri; but the City owners do and Ranieri said he was told that even if the worst happened and City were relegated, they still believed in him.

'Yes I thought that was unbelievable,' said Ranieri. 'He asked me just one question: "If we go down you stay with us?" That was unbelievable.'

They may have been prepared for the worst, but City's progress under Ranieri was going better than anyone could have imagined.

In an interview in his native tongue Ranieri would eloquently sum up what he and City were managing to do.

'In an era when money counts for everything, I think we give hope to everybody.'

WHEN YOU'RE SMILING

What a difference twelve months had made to the fortunes of Leicester City.

Christmas 2014 was bleak for City fans. There wasn't much cause for rejoicing as their team sat rock bottom of the Premier League with just ten points on the board from the first 17 games. They were five points adrift of safety and the odds were stacked against them. Only West Bromwich Albion in 2004/05 and Sunderland in 2013/14 had managed to survive having been bottom at Christmas.

A year on and City's stunning 3-2 victory over Everton at Goodison Park, courtesy of two Riyad Mahrez penalties and another tenacious goal from Shinji Okazaki, meant Claudio Ranieri's men would be top of the Premier League at Christmas. Talk about a Christmas miracle (although resurrections of such biblical proportions are usually part of the Easter story).

The city of Leicester had recently caught the attention of the world's media when the skeletal remains of Richard III – one of the most controversial monarchs in the nation's history, whose death at the Battle of Bosworth changed the course of the English monarchy, marking the end of the Plantagenets and the start of the Tudor dynasty – had been found buried under a city centre car park (beneath a parking spot that bore the letter R).

After being killed in battle with Henry Tudor his body had been buried at Greyfriars Church in Leicester, close to the battlefield. The church was later demolished. After being discovered in 2012 and then identified, Richard's remains were reburied at Leicester Cathedral and media from around the world came to watch the procession and ceremonies around Leicestershire.

Now the media spotlight was on City, and it was shining even brighter than it did for a king of England. The interest in Jamie Vardy, Riyad Mahrez, Claudio Ranieri and the rest was insatiable. Everyone wanted to know how it was possible that a team that had been bottom of the league at the start of the year would now be top at the start of the next?

Trying to find rational explanations was proving difficult because this had never happened before, so some looked for irrational, even supernatural reasons to explain how this had come about. Some noted that City's incredible reversal of fortunes began after Richard's reburial and surmised that the king was rewarding the city of Leicester for the dignified way he was treated by watching over the city's beloved football team from the grave.

Leicestershire is a county of stark contrast. It is a large, rural county with many small villages and towns, but in the centre is one modern, multicultural city, a thriving hub amidst the tranquillity of the rest of the county. It is like a super model who has a mole on her face, but not an ugly mole – Leicestershire is the Cindy Crawford of counties.

At the heart of the city are the sports clubs which carry the city's name. The Leicester Tigers rugby club is among the most famous in the European game. (In fact, when Mahrez first heard of Leicester's interest, the only sports club he had heard of from the city were the Tigers; he thought some terrible mistake had been made.) Founded in 1880, the Tigers have won the English Premiership ten times since its formation in 1987 and have been European champions twice. The county cricket club has won the County Championship three times as well as eight other titles, while the Leicester Riders basketball club, the oldest in the country, having been formed in 1967, has won several titles, moving to its own purpose-built arena in 2016. The Leicester Lions speedway team are also competing in the English Elite League.

Then there is Leicester City. While the football club has not exactly enjoyed a trophy-laden history since being formed as Leicester Fosse in 1884, it is beloved in the community as a source of identity and pride. Nearly every-one in Leicestershire supports City and when City are doing well people from Leicester have a spring in their step, puff their chests out and are not shy in displaying their pride that they are from Leicester.

The club anthem is the old Louis Armstrong classic 'When You're Smiling', sung with gusto and at breakneck speed by the Blue Army at grounds around the country. It seems to have been transferred to the Filbert Street terraces in the 1960s by the regulars of the Three Cranes pub, now long gone, in Humberstone Gate. They used to sing it in the pub before matches and took it with them to the game. The line about the whole world smiling with you could not have been more appropriate in 2015/16 because the watching world were smiling just as broadly as the people of Leicester as their football team sat proudly at the top of the table.

At Everton, City had made it 18 consecutive Premier League games in which they had scored, and either Vardy or Mahrez had been on the scoresheet in every one. That was an astonishing statistic that emphasised their importance to City. City were missing two key men for that game: defender Robert Huth, through suspension, and injured midfielder Danny Drinkwater, who watched City beat the Toffees amidst the Blue Army in the away section. Several times they would break out the Drinkwater song in tribute, even if he wasn't on the pitch.

Despite those absences, City were still able to come away with the victory, with Mahrez and Vardy at the heart of City's exhilarating attacking play. Shinji Okazaki earned the penalty which Mahrez converted for the first goal, before Romelu Lukaku equalised for the hosts. Then Mahrez played Vardy through and after he was tripped by goalkeeper Tim

Howard, Mahrez kept his cool to slot home his second penalty of the day and his sixth goal in three games. Vardy then teed up Okazaki unselfishly for City's third goal. Kevin Mirallas scored a late second for the Toffees, but it was too little too late for Roberto Martinez's men.

City were back up the M6 to Merseyside a week later for the Boxing Day clash with Liverpool at Anfield, and there were the first real signs that teams were now starting to take City very seriously. Now sides were starting to show City much more respect, and in particular Mahrez and Vardy.

Jürgen Klopp had enjoyed considerable success at Borussia Dortmund with a brand of high-energy, high-pressing counter-attacking that City were now adopting with great joy. In fact, during one of his spells out of the game Ranieri had been to watch some Dortmund training sessions and games, and now he was using what he had learned at City. However, it was Klopp who would prove he was still the master of this style of play as Liverpool inflicted only the second defeat of the season on City. From the first whistle the Reds were straight at City's throats and when Mahrez touched the ball for the first time he was surrounded by three red shirts. Vardy was finding time and space equally difficult to come by. Christian Benteke grabbed what would prove to be the winner in the second half to inflict City's first away defeat since losing at Tottenham Hotspur in March and while there was no shortage of effort or commitment from City, they lacked the spark that had lit up the Premier League since the start of the campaign.

'We didn't start to play until late on. I don't know why,' said Ranieri afterwards. 'We looked anxious and nervous.'

Before Christmas, City's lead had been cut to two points by Arsenal after their win over Manchester City, who were to be Leicester's next opponents at the King Power Stadium.

The Gunners then missed an opportunity to overtake the Foxes as they were thumped 4-0 away at Southampton on Boxing Day, but Arsène Wenger's inconsistent side did leap-frog Leicester two days later, taking a one-point lead with a home victory over Bournemouth.

There were just four points separating the top four of Arsenal, Leicester, Tottenham Hotspur and Manchester City, and the Citizens would also go above the Foxes if they could claim victory at the King Power Stadium on 29 December. After the defeat at Liverpool and the Gunners taking top spot, Ranieri's men were again being written off.

City had not beaten the Citizens on home soil for 27 years when Manuel Pellegrini's pre-season title favourites arrived at the King Power Stadium, but there was still an air of optimism around the stadium, summed up by vice-chairman Aiyawatt Srivaddhanaprabha's notes in *City*, the official matchday magazine.

'I don't think there were many fans who would have expected us to lead the Premier League table at Christmas, but Claudio, his players and staff have earned their place among the most consistent teams in the division,' he wrote. 'It's been one of the many highlights from 2015 – the amazing escape of last season, the fantastic start to this one, club records broken, Premier League records broken and moments that will live with us all for a long time. You, the fans, have all been a huge part of it and Leicester City heads into 2016 in better shape than it has ever been.'

There was nothing between the two sides on the night. In fact, the Foxes created more chances to score but on this occasion Vardy couldn't provide the final, killer touch. However, the result moved Leicester back level with Arsenal at the top of the table, second only on goal difference at the halfway point of the season.

'It has been an incredible year, last season and now this season,' said skipper Wes Morgan after the game. 'We have something to be proud of. We have done extremely well and set a standard for ourselves now that we want to maintain. We have shown how good we can be as a team.

'We have played everyone now and we have shown we are more than capable of playing up there with the best of them.

'We are halfway now and we want to push on in the second half of the season.'

LEICESTER MERCURY BLOG, 30 DECEMBER 2015
HALF-TIME REVIEW

Well, here we are at the halfway stage of the season and still Leicester City are riding high in the Premier League.

Who would have believed it was possible? Perhaps not even Claudio Ranieri and his players could have predicted they would be sat level on points with leaders Arsenal going into 2016.

City are amazingly three points ahead of title favourites Manchester City, nine above Manchester United, who have lifted the Premier League trophy 13 times, 12 ahead of Liverpool and 19 ahead of reigning champions Chelsea.

Incredible, astonishing, extraordinary, unbelievable – take your pick of your favourite superlative to describe the first half of a campaign that potentially could be one of the greatest in the club's history.

The question now is can they sustain it? Can City kick on again in 2016?

Much of that may depend on what happens over the next month.

The January transfer window opens on Saturday and while a lot of the attention will be on the possibility of other clubs trying to steal away City's prize assets, it is on the players that potentially could be coming in that I am more focused.

I do not have any fears that City will sell Jamie Vardy, Riyad Mahrez or any of their other influential players, and I don't think fringe players like Gökhan Inler or Andrej Kramarić, who haven't had much pitch time this season, will be allowed to leave either until City have brought in replacements.

The window is for strengthening your squad, not weakening it.

With that in mind – and despite Claudio Ranieri's public statements that he is not looking to bring in any players to avoid the risk of destabilising the harmony within his squad – I do believe City need to strengthen.

City have done fantastically well but in the last two performances there have been signs of fatigue as the high-octane, fast-flowing style of play has started to take its toll physically on one or two who have played in every game.

It will be difficult to sustain that style of play for an entire 38 games without one or two reinforcements.

Another factor will be pressure. So far City have played without any expectation and with freedom. This has been a fantastic ride and they have looked like they have enjoyed every minute.

However, now they are in completely uncharted water and tension can creep in because, unlike before, they now have something to lose.

The mantra has been 'take each game as it comes and reach 40 points'. They now have to adjust their sights and aim a little higher.

City have put themselves in a wonderful position and they have a golden opportunity to achieve something special, and opportunities like this don't come along all the time.

It is time for City to seize it by strengthening when they are at their strongest.

Of course, City fans will have to put up with plenty of speculation regarding Vardy and Mahrez so expect the transfer window equivalent of the hokey cokey.

We saw it this week with one report that Manchester City were preparing a £30 million bid for Vardy followed two days later by another national newspaper contradicting that claim with a denial from Manchester City that they are in for Vardy.

'A bid has gone in, a bid has gone out, in, out, shake it all about!'

Hopefully, the speculation won't unsettle any of the camp. There has been plenty of it already and it hasn't had an effect yet.

DECEMBER SUMMARY

Competition	Date	Fixture
Premier League	Sat 5 Dec	Swansea 0-3 Leicester
Premier League	Mon 14 Dec	Leicester 2-1 Chelsea
Premier League	Sat 19 Dec	Everton 2-3 Leicester
Premier League	Sat 26 Dec	Liverpool 1-0 Leicester
Premier League	Tue 29 Dec	Leicester 0-0 Man City

The Foxes came through a gruelling Christmas schedule to finish the year joint top:

33-1 – 5 December (after winning at Swansea)

20-1 – 14 December (after winning at home to Chelsea)

12-1 – 27 December (the day after losing at Liverpool)

JANUARY 2016

		P	W	D	L	GF	GA	GD	Pts
1	Arsenal	19	12	3	4	33	18	15	39
2	Leicester City	19	11	6	2	37	25	12	39
3	Manchester City	19	11	3	5	37	20	17	36
4	Tottenham Hotspur	19	9	8	2	33	15	18	35

Standings on 1 January

THE TOTTENHAM TRILOGY

What Leicester City had achieved in the first half of the season was a miracle, manager Claudio Ranieri said at the halfway stage.

'I think what we did is a miracle, but if we finish in the top four it is not a miracle, it something bigger – out of this galaxy. What we are doing is a miracle so far but you imagine if we continue it is something unbelievable,' he said.

'I came at the right moment because they were down all of last season and then the last two months [of last season] they were like a volcano. There was an explosion and then this explosion continues. I don't know how this is possible.

'This is a crazy league this year. We made a fantastic half-season, it is unbelievable what we are doing but now we must continue this way.'

That was exactly what City were trying – and expected – to do when they kicked-off the second half of the season at home to AFC Bournemouth.

There hadn't been many disappointments during the first half of the season. There weren't many occasions when City fans left the stadium with the sick feeling in the pit of their stomachs. Even after the defeats to Arsenal and Liverpool, there wasn't any real negativity. Against the Gunners City had simply faced a side on a day where everything clicked, while there is never any shame in losing a tight game at Anfield.

It was a very different matter when City faced AFC Bournemouth at the King Power Stadium for their New Year fixture. For starters, Leicester's incredible first half of the campaign had raised expectations enormously. They were now going into games as favourites to win. That hadn't been the case earlier in the season, even on home soil. In fact, former Liverpool defender and now *Match of the Day* pundit Mark Lawrenson, in his weekly predictions column on the BBC website, had consistently forecast defeats for Leicester, to such an extent that, had all his predictions come true, City would now have been facing Bournemouth in a relegation battle, rather than trying to maintain a title challenge.

City were expected to beat Eddie Howe's Premier League new boys, but that didn't mean they were underestimating the Cherries. They had shown in the first game at the Vitality Stadium how good a side they were. City had needed a late Vardy penalty to claim a point. Howe had lost several key players to injury since then, including former Foxes winger Max Gradel and main striker Callum Wilson, but Bournemouth were still putting up a valiant fight to stay in the Premier League.

Ranieri brought Leonardo Ulloa into the side at the expense of Gökhan Inler, who had been drafted in as an extra midfielder against Manchester City but was now sacrificed as Ranieri opted for more attacking potency. However, it was to be an afternoon of frustration for City, and especially for Riyad Mahrez. Mahrez saw his second-half penalty saved by Artur Boruc and despite playing against ten men for the final 30 minutes after Bournemouth captain Simon Francis was sent off for tripping Vardy for the spot-kick, City could not force a winner, being guilty of some wasteful finishing – as the Cherries had also been in the first half. Joshua King and Dan Gosling missed great chances for the visitors early on but City couldn't take advantage of their failure to convert them: Vardy struck the inside of the post and a number of good opportunities were wasted.

It is interesting how a point can be perceived. When City snatched a draw at Bournemouth with Vardy's late penalty it was celebrated like a victory by the City fans. It was the same outcome this time but after Mahrez's penalty miss it felt like a defeat, two points thrown away, an opportunity missed.

It was now three games without a goal for City but the point took them to the 40-point mark Ranieri had targeted from the outset. After the game he, surprisingly, said it was time for his players to break out the champagne.

'We have 40 points and kept a clean sheet, so there is champagne for my players,' he said. 'Maybe the chairman pays for the champagne. I paid for the pizza!'

Vardy had now gone four games without a goal, his longest barren run of the season, and Ranieri admitted at some point he would need a rest to be able to maintain his high-octane performances. Vardy, in fact, needed more than a rest: he needed surgery to correct a niggling groin injury he had been carrying and so was ruled out of the FA Cup third-round clash with Spurs at White Hart Lane.

Spurs would become very familiar to City as this would be the first of a trilogy of fixtures against the north London club – although not much could be gleaned from the first game as both managers made substantial changes to their start-ing line-ups, sparking more debate about how the famous competition was perceived by modern clubs and managers.

There is a growing perception that the enormous financial rewards of the Premier League now outweigh the romance of a cup run and a trip to Wembley to such an extent that managers now choose to play much-weakened teams in the cup and prioritise the league. City and Spurs did just that. With one eye on the league clash between the two clubs at White Hart Lane just three days later, City made eight changes, including giving debuts to new sign-ing Demarai Gray and 19-year-old left-back Ben Chilwell, while Spurs made six; but that didn't mean the fans were short-changed. In fact, they were treated to a thriller.

City had won an entertaining encounter in the fourth round at White Hart Lane the season before after coming from behind, and they would have to do the same again now after Christian Eriksen fired the hosts in front after nine minutes.

The debutants Gray and Chilwell would both play a prominent role, as it was from Gray's corner that Marcin Wasilewski headed City's equaliser, and in the second half it was Chilwell who played Okazaki through for the Japan international to bundle the ball home after his first effort was blocked.

However, there was a controversial finale as Nathan Dyer was penalised for handball when he was trying to stop Danny Rose's surging run into the box. The ball bounced up off his heel and, as he turned to look for the ball, it hit his hand. City felt hard done by by referee Robert Madley, but Harry Kane duly converted the spot-kick to level the scores at 2-2, meaning City would now have to face Spurs again in the replay at the King Power Stadium, ten days later.

The one positive was that it meant more opportunities for the players who had struggled to break into Ranieri's regular starting line-up. The replay would provide valuable pitch time for Inler, Wasilewski and Dyer. There had been a lot of expectation when Inler arrived but it was clear from the start that he would need more time to adapt to the very different demands of the Premier League. In Italy the game is played at a much slower pace than in England, and City's style in particular would require Inler to play at a very high tempo. There was no question Inler was a class player on the ball and he had looked every inch the international when he captained Switzerland against England at Wembley earlier in the season, but there wasn't time to take a touch and put your foot on the ball when City were launching a lightning counter-attack. City couldn't afford for any part of their well-oiled speed machine to be running slowly. The question wasn't whether Inler was a good player, it was just whether he could adapt quickly enough.

Wasilewski is a popular figure among City fans. His no-nonsense, uncompromising approach to defending earned him the nickname the Polish Tank. He had recovered from a horrendous broken leg, which could have ended his career, while playing for Anderlecht and fought his way back to help City reach the Premier League. He had then partnered Wes Morgan superbly as City pulled off the Great Escape.

Wasilewski is a man of few words. In fact, he doesn't do media at all. We tried, once, when he first joined the club. BBC Radio Leicester reporter Jason Bourne was asking the questions and the interview was being filmed, but it didn't go well. At the time his English was limited. I had spoken to Wasilewski briefly and it was okay as I kept my questions simple. He could stop and ask for me to repeat the question, so he was more comfortable – that's the advantage of being a written journalist. There was no microphone or camera so he was more relaxed. Although Jason was trying his best, it was a distinctly more uncomfortable Wasilewski. After a few questions Jason asked Wasilewski about how he would cope with 'the rigours' of English football. Wasilewski looked around, bewildered, and just walked off. No one tried to stop him. No one was brave enough.

I haven't spoken to Wasilewski since then. I don't think any English journalist has. He marches through the Mixed Zones with his eyes fixed on his destination, avoiding any possibility of making eye contact with a journalist and risking drawing a question. I have never heard anyone try to ask him one either. Now I know why he is the Polish Tank: not because he goes through opposition strikers, but because he is unstoppable in Mixed Zones.

Three days later, still smarting from the late penalty decision in the cup tie, City were back down 'the Lane' for the league clash, and it was to be another tight affair between two sides who would go on to become genuine and unlikely title rivals. Both sides were back to full strength and City were boosted by the return of Vardy just eight days after undergoing surgery on his groin. Ranieri would admit after the game that the injury had been hampering Vardy for over a month and he had been unable to train effectively, which explained why he had uncharacteristically been on a four-game barren run in front of goal. However, it wasn't Vardy who would be City's goalscoring hero on this occasion: it was the unlikely figure of Robert Huth who would steal the headlines with a second-half winner.

The press bench at White Hart Lane is unique because it is at pitch level and immediately behind where the substitutes and staff sit, allowing a fascinating, up-close insight into the almost animalistic behaviour of managers and coaches. Sometimes it is like watching a wildlife show as the managers prowl along the edge of the technical area like caged jungle cats, occasionally bursting into frantic animation when something riles them. Mauricio Pochettino, whose suit trousers seemed on this occasion to hover several inches above his shoes like those of a schoolboy after a growth spurt, comes from Latin stock and there was no hiding his emotion when something angered him, whether that was the referee or his own players. His assistant, Jesús Pérez, would occasionally wander out to issue a few orders as well.

Craig Shakespeare would do the same in the opposite technical area but his big role during a game was to be City's mediator with the fourth official. His calm demeanour made him perfect for the task – he could pass on Ranieri's, and previously Nigel Pearson's, displeasure at a decision in a diplomatic yet forceful and quizzical way. On this day at White Hart Lane, the fourth official had positioned himself at the end of the tunnel and it was enlightening to watch how many times he was called upon to answer a query from one bench or the other. On the face of it the official's main job appears to be to hold up the LED board to signal a substitution, but it is clear that he also has a major role as a psychological punching bag for managers.

White Hart Lane has offered other insights during previous visits. The season before, Pearson had wandered down the tunnel during the warm-up and stopped for a chat. He admitted he found himself at a loose end in the minutes before a game. He had delivered his team talk and it was over to his assistants and the fitness coaches to get the players prepared physically for the game. He had nothing to do, so he talked me through his City line-up for that game instead. A journalist couldn't interact with a manager like that at any other ground.

The drawback, though, of the press bench position is that it can give you a misleading impression of events on the pitch. On this day, it appeared that Huth had leapt like the proverbial salmon above the Spurs defence to power home his header from Christian Fuchs' corner. In fact, as the City fans in the away end behind the goal would point out on social media, Huth had eluded his marker and didn't even have to jump to plant his bullet header past Hugo Lloris.

Huth had become a cult figure at City since his loan arrival the previous season. A booming cry of 'Huuuuuuuuuth', which could be mistaken for booing at first, would ring out whenever he did something impressive, which was pretty regular. He didn't speak to the media very often – he didn't want to answer the same questions repeatedly – but his teammates would talk of a man who loved a laugh and had an incredibly dry sense of humour.

A no-nonsense defender, the German has a commanding presence and it was no coincidence that the sloppy goals City had been conceding had dried up since his arrival. Captain Wes Morgan had become a much better defender alongside him too. He had become one of City's key signings, and yet, like many of his teammates, he was a player who had become surplus to requirements at other clubs, in his case Chelsea and then Stoke City. Fans of both clubs would look at Huth's dominant performances for Leicester and ask, 'Why did we let him go?'

Huth had been signed as a youth by then-Chelsea boss Ranieri from FC Union Berlin in 2001 and made his first team debut at 17, but while he was part of the squad that won two Premier League titles, it wasn't enough. His lack of first-team opportunities following the emergence of John Terry left him feeling his departure was inevitable. He knew it was unlikely that he would be challenging for the biggest prize in English football again as he moved to Middlesbrough, Stoke City and then to Leicester, but he felt he couldn't develop into the player he has become without regular first-team football.

'I didn't expect this,' Huth would say in a rare interview later in the season. 'To be playing for a club like Chelsea is a big thing but it wasn't right for me at the time. It wasn't good enough to not be getting in the team at a time when they were winning titles and trophies. I just needed to play. That was the end of it. I learned some huge things there but the club was going one way and I wasn't sticking with the quality they were bringing in. It was the natural thing to move on.'

It may have been a gamble to leave a Chelsea squad that had emerged into a European power but Huth was now reaping his reward for such a bold move, although he admits that never in his wildest dreams did he expect City to be challenging at the top of the league. When he had arrived on loan the previous season, City had been bottom of the table and looking odds-on for relegation. Now, with just five games remaining, City were seven points clear at the top. It represented a remarkable transformation.

'I have never experienced anything like it,' said Huth. 'It is some turnaround. You just don't expect a turnaround that quick. Teams take years and years to be established and have success in the Premier League.

'We started off just to be safe this season. We started off looking at getting 38 or 40 points. That was our focus from day one. We had no ambitions for the top ten or anything like that, it was just to stay in the league and then go from there.

'We have got a chance, yes. I am loving it. I have never won so many games in one season, two if you count the end of last season. It is fun. You can see the enjoyment of the lads when they come off the pitch. It is exciting and fun to be here.'

Now Huth was City's match-winner at White Hart Lane. How big a goal, and a victory, it would prove to be would become apparent as the season progressed.

City were second in the table behind Arsenal but still no one really believed they could go on to become English champions, including Ranieri, who admitted he had been receiving advice from his wife.

'I get asked all the time, "Can you win the title?",' he said. 'My wife says "Claudio, slow down. The journalists want to push you, slow down." It's easy to say, "Yes, Leicester can fight for the title" but of course I think they don't believe. They say Arsenal, Tottenham, United, Manchester City, Chelsea, who are used to fighting for the title, will fight. They say, "Leicester is there, but can they arrive at the end and fight?" Nobody knows and we don't have the pedigree to say, "Yes, Leicester is there" so far. At the moment, no. Everybody says, "Sooner or later they will slow down." That is normal. If little Leicester slow down that's normal but it's not normal what Leicester are doing. It's unbelievable.'

Three days later it seemed the doubters were justified as City failed to beat struggling Aston Villa at Villa Park. Villa had endured a terrible season and were rock bottom with just 11 points on the board going into the game. Everywhere around Villa Park there are reminders of the days when they were English and European champions, but those days seemed a long, long time ago now.

The rot had been setting in for several seasons but Tim Sherwood had managed to keep them up the season before. It seemed it had only delayed the inevitable. Sherwood had been sacked after just ten league games of the season, and instead of turning to an experienced manager, battle-hardened from relegation scraps, Villa had turned to Frenchman Rémy Garde, a man with no experience of managing in England, let alone the Premier League.

What Villa had needed was a man with recent history of fighting a successful battle against relegation, a man who had proven again and again that he could stop the rot at a club on the slide – a man like Nigel Pearson. Pearson had halted the decline at both Leicester and Hull City and got both clubs moving in the right direction again after relegations. He had pulled off the Great Escape just months before, but he wasn't approached by Villa's hierarchy, who were looking increasingly to their own supporters as though they didn't know what they were doing.

The demise of the once-proud Midland giants would continue but they would have a small lift after snatching a draw against City. Shinji Okazaki had put City ahead, bundling the ball over the line in typical fashion as the visitors dominated the game at a muted Villa Park, and Riyad Mahrez had the chance to really capitalise on the air of impending doom around the ground when City were awarded a penalty, but Mark Bunn guessed the right way to keep his team in the game. City continued to create chances but failed to take them and were eventually punished by substitute Rudy Gestede, who had been a scourge of Leicester on many occasions while with Cardiff City in the Championship. It was two points dropped, even though the point briefly took City back into top spot with the Gunners playing the next day.

Okazaki spoke to the media afterwards with one of the Japanese press pack translating, and he revealed how much he had settled in England. 'I like fish and chips,' he said. 'I have them sometimes, maybe once every two weeks, then I am happy. Now I have scored I want some fish and chips – it is better than pizza. This is unbelievable. I am happy and Leicester is a strong team like a family. Top of the table? I don't know if it will last but we take it game by game.'

The games were certainly coming thick and fast for City – although mostly against the same opposition. Spurs were in town four days after the disappointment of the Villa stalemate for the cup replay – the fourth meeting between the two rivals in six months. The previous three had all been close, keenly contested encounters, resulting in two draws and a tight win for City. The two sides, and squads, could hardly be separated in terms of quality. Even after liberal rotation there wasn't much to choose between them.

Both sides announced eight changes, although that became nine in City's case as Ritchie De Laet pulled out of the warm-up. There were home debuts for Gray and Chilwell, who had been so impressive in the first game.

Chances were at a premium but Spurs just shaded the first half and led through Son Heung-min's impressive finish. Ranieri demonstrated again that the visit of Stoke City at the weekend was the priority and withdrew Danny Drinkwater at half-time, and Nacer Chadli booked Spurs' passage into the fourth round, where they would face Colchester United, with a second goal midway through the half.

Spurs deserved to go through on the night, although the controversial nature of how they had earned a replay in the first place still rankled with City fans. However, they weren't too downcast. City have suffered many disappointments in the FA Cup throughout their history and it has been a dream of the Blue Army to one day see a City skipper hold aloft that trophy, which has always eluded the club; but it felt like this season there were even bigger fish to fry.

Now City were out of all the cup competitions they only had one thing to focus on – the pursuit of a Champions League place and, possibly, an even greater prize.

LEICESTER MERCURY BLOG, 28 JANUARY 2016
DANIEL AMARTEY SIGNS FOR CITY

It isn't often I get excited about a new Leicester City signing but there is something intriguing about Daniel Amartey.

I have to confess, when I first was told of City's interest in the Ghana international in the summer I replied, 'Who?'

I don't watch much Scandinavian football and Amartey had not yet hit the international stage.

But since City returned for Amartey, who only turned 21

last month, I have been trying to find out more about him, and I have liked what I have heard and seen.

YouTube clips can be misleading about a player's ability as they generally don't give you a true picture of their attributes, but if Amartey turns out to be as good as his clips suggest, City have signed themselves one hell of a prospect who ticks all the boxes of what I believe City look for in a player.

For a start he is young and will be able to develop within the City squad, growing as City hopefully grow into a Premier League force.

He is a great athlete too. Big, strong and fast, it is not hard to see why he is so versatile, being able to use those attributes at centre-back, right-back and centre midfield.

He is good in the air and also has one hell of a shot on him, judging by some of the goals he has scored.

Plus, at £5 million, his signature doesn't break the bank and if he develops as expected he will command much more than that. £5 million is a lot of money in the real world but in the Premier League it is peanuts.

Of course, this is all ifs and buts, and we will only really know if City have unearthed another gem when we see Amartey in action over a number of games.

THE WORLD STARTS TO BELIEVE
IN THE UNBELIEVABLE

Every time questions had been asked of Leicester City they had answered them.

After their heavy defeat to Arsenal, the doubters had said City would fall away and slip back into the pack, where they were perceived to belong.

It was the same after Christmas, following the defeat to Liverpool, when they had drawn 0-0 at home with Manchester City and AFC Bournemouth. Many had thought the wheels were about to fall off the Leicester bandwagon.

They were wrong. City had been able to regroup and regain their momentum, but now they faced a run of fixtures which would be their biggest test of the season.

Nigel Pearson once said he would look at the season in blocks of fixtures and set points targets for each group of games. That is what supporters tend to do as well. And that was exactly the approach as City went into a run of four games which could potentially make or break their season.

City were to entertain Stoke City and Liverpool at the King Power Stadium before heading out for the extremely difficult away games at Manchester City and Arsenal, two of the pre-season title favourites and now, remarkably, two of City's main rivals.

City had won just one of their previous five games and the goals had dried up for their key attacking players. Vardy hadn't scored in his previous seven games, while it had been five since Mahrez had scored. He had also missed the last two penalties, which had proved costly against Bournemouth and Aston Villa. Was the pressure starting to get to them? Was the weight of expectation for them to deliver every week becoming too much? Ranieri was certainly doing everything he could to relieve any pressure.

'It's important they don't feel the pressure because I don't give pressure,' he said. 'For me it's not important. Until now he [Vardy] was a normal player, but now he is our spotlight. You say Leicester, you say Vardy, or Mahrez. These two guys find this pressure in their lives and it is good to bring this pressure.'

Ranieri tried to relieve any perceived pressure by refusing to even contemplate the idea that they were emerging as Champions League and title contenders. It wasn't that his side were punching way above their weight, it was because the big hitters were below par, he stressed.

'It is a crazy season, yes, but not only for Leicester but for all the teams,' he said. 'Last season started with Chelsea and ended with Chelsea at the top. This season we are fighting, but it's not normal. This is something special and we want to fight for something special.

'Maybe I'm sure next season we are better but maybe we don't fight for the top four. That is crazy, this league is crazy. Yes we are closing the gap. The table says there is no gap but everybody who knows football knows there is a big gap between Leicester and the other teams.'

City were up against a Potters side having another excellent season in the league and Mark Hughes's men had the second leg of the Capital One Cup semi-final against Liverpool on the horizon too. Stoke were looking to claw back a one-goal deficit at Anfield and they may have had one eye on that game when they turned up at the King Power Stadium. In-form winger Marko Arnautović was left out because of a hamstring injury, but he was fit to start at Liverpool three days later.

Regardless, it was an emphatic performance from Leicester as they beat the Potters convincingly, 3-0, to move back above Arsenal, who would lose to Chelsea the following evening. A deflected strike from Danny Drinkwater put City ahead in the first half before second-half goals from Vardy and Leonardo Ulloa completed the win. It was the perfect riposte to those who were predicting the bubble would burst.

Vardy and Mahrez looked back to their best. Vardy, after his groin surgery, said he hadn't felt as fit and fresh for weeks, and his goal was vintage Vardy as he ran off the shoulder of the last defender to latch on to a superbly timed pass before rounding keeper Jack Butland and rolling the ball into the empty net. Mahrez also started to show signs that his confidence was returning after those two saved penalties; the Algerian wizard produced a few moments of magic, most notably an audacious nutmeg on Philipp Wollscheid before teeing up substitute Ulloa for City's third goal.

'I think it does help when people write us off,' said man of the match Drinkwater. 'There has not been much negative stuff around us this season, but the boys will talk about it [and] if a team or whoever has been talking badly of us then we will be the first ones looking to put it right.'

Christian Fuchs echoed Drinkwater's sentiment. 'People writing us off isn't a topic for us. We know there's a lot of writing about us outside the club and the press can talk and assume things but we focus on our work and we do it well.'

City had plenty of time to contemplate the tricky trio of fixtures that lay before them after their FA Cup exit presented them with a free weekend, but Ranieri didn't want reminding of what lay in wait for his side. He said City were prepared for the worst.

'I told the players today in the briefing that the month of February is very, very tough,' he said. 'It's important to be top of the league because after, if a bad moment arrives, we are strong enough to get over this bad moment.

'This is a strange league. The big teams are not at the top. There is Leicester. What happened? I don't know, but I want to stay there. Now the players will have three days off so they can clear their minds and then when they come back we work hard because this league is very exciting for us.'

Leicester had a ten-point buffer between themselves and Manchester United in fifth spot and the prospect of

Champions League football, for the first time in the club's history, was becoming increasingly possible, even if the Foxes did suffer the predicted blip.

However, there was no sign of City tensing up and defender Robert Huth said the Leicester camp was extremely relaxed ahead of the challenging sequence of games. In fact, he said, that hadn't changed from the previous season when they were deeply embroiled in the fight for survival.

'You can see in training everyday how relaxed we are,' he said. 'It helps when you've won as many games as we have so far that we get to laugh, but even when I came here last year everyone was so happy. I was thinking, "What's going on, you're bottom of the league and the players are having fun and playing jokes." I wasn't used to it but it's clearly worked because we've stayed together in tight situations and that's exactly what we have been doing – having fun as a group. We're 25 mates and more with the staff included. You can see it. It's just a formula that works at the moment.'

THE TRIALS AND TRIBULATION
OF THE TRANSFER WINDOW

The transfer window had been eagerly awaited by Leicester City fans, keen to see whether their club were going to stick or twist, although there was still some trepidation as the previous few months had been dominated by speculation that City would struggle to hold on to their prize assets.

City fans knew their club was in a strong, but surprising, position in the league and had a great opportunity of Champions League qualification, at the very least. If they really went for it perhaps an even greater prize could be possible, they thought. If they could keep hold of Jamie Vardy and Riyad Mahrez, and bring in a few new additions, City would be in great shape for the rest of the campaign.

Did City have the strength in depth and the quality throughout the squad to be able to stay the course? Many City fans wanted Ranieri to spend big to bring in at least one player of proven quality who could make a big impact in the second half of the season. There were areas of the team that did need strengthening: another striker to supplement Jamie Vardy, Leonardo Ulloa and Shinji Okazaki seemed to be the biggest priority, especially as Andrej Kramarić looked to be completely out in the cold, with Ranieri even stating he felt he would be better served going out on loan. He eventually did.

As well as the fact that the January transfer window is notoriously difficult to deal effectively in, the conundrum for Ranieri was that he felt there was a risk of any new arrivals rocking the boat and affecting the fantastic team spirit and camaraderie within the squad. 'We have a very good squad with good mentality,' he said. 'They are very friendly; this is our strength, to be close to each other. They do not want to break this.'

The big concern, however, wasn't who could potentially be coming in and what impact that could have, but who could be heading out. There had hardly been a day that had gone by in the build-up to the opening of the window that a story hadn't been published linking either Vardy or Mahrez with some of the biggest clubs in world football. Spanish giants Real Madrid, Manchester United and Barcelona were after Mahrez, according to the reports, while Vardy's goal-scoring form had attracted strong interest from Chelsea, among many others, the national newspapers said.

Even though both players said they had no desire to leave City, the rumours continued, meaning City fans couldn't relax. Football fans get used to proclamations of loyalty from players, who kiss the badge after they score and say they love the club only to jump ship shortly afterwards, but when Mahrez and Vardy both said they wanted to stay at City it was sincere.

'It would be best for me to stay,' Mahrez told French news outlet BFM TV. 'I will not leave in January; it would not be good for my team if I left. If you lose a player like me or Kanté, Jamie Vardy, it may penalise the team. I prefer to continue with the team until the end of the year.' Vardy was equally dismissive of the reports and would soon commit his immediate future to the club by signing a new, lucrative contract. 'You have seen what is going on at this club; it is building in a way they want to be challenging at the top all the time,' said Vardy.

When asked if he was concerned he was about to lose his two star men, Ranieri was adamant no one from City would be leaving who he didn't want to go. 'I think nobody goes from Leicester,' he said. 'We are a solid team and we want to continue together with everybody. They have said they want to stay with us and fight until the end and build with me and the chairman and our fans a big Leicester. They have very good potential but they must stay with us if they want to achieve big things because maybe Leicester in two or three years could be a very big team. We don't need the money, just good players to try to achieve our dream and the dream of our fans. Besides, the other clubs don't have enough money to buy them.'

While the issue would constantly be bubbling away, attention turned to recruitment. Ranieri and City's new lofty status in the table would certainly help their cause: City were now a much more attractive proposition for potential targets.

'Maybe now a lot of people say "Oh, Leicester are top of the league" [and] maybe they change their mind,' said Ranieri. 'Maybe at the beginning or in June when we tried to bring in some players they thought "Oh no, Leicester. They were almost relegated last season. It is not so good." Perhaps the agents are also now thinking "Oh, Leicester!".

'Our recruitment department look every day around the world at a lot of players. At this moment we will continue with our players. When the window opens maybe we will do something and then you will know afterwards what happened.'

City fans didn't have to wait long as the club completed the signing of Birmingham City's rising young winger Demarai Gray as the window opened. Gray had been on City's radar for a considerable time. The club had tried to sign him in the summer, triggering a clause in his contract, but the 19-year-old admirably wanted to stay for the time being with Birmingham, where he was a regular starter. Now the lure of the Premier League was too much and Leicester again triggered the £3.7 million release clause in his contract to sign him. He would make his debut almost immediately, in the FA Cup tie at Tottenham Hotspur.

The recruitment process at City is incredibly thorough and the scouts, led by head of recruitment Steve Walsh, are meticulous in their scouting. They look at hours of video footage of each player as well as sending scouts to watch the player live, before Walsh himself goes to see the player in the flesh. They look at all the statistical data available too. A classic example of the statistical analysis was N'Golo Kanté's stats on tackles made and won cleanly, which was a big factor in their decision to sign him. They also look at the player's background, his lifestyle, his attitude and his personality. Is he hungry and driven? Will this player fit into the group? It is a lengthy process and one of the major reasons why knowledge of City's potential targets is sometimes in the public domain for such a long time. That was certainly true of the two major signings they made during January 2016, Gray and Daniel Amartey.

Amartey was another City target who they had tried to sign in the previous transfer window, but issues over a work permit for the Ghanaian had made the deal tricky and City eventually pulled out. Now the 21-year-old was a full Ghana international and the situation was a lot more favourable.

Unlike in England, transfer deals are announced to the stock exchange in Denmark so City's pursuit of Amartey was in the public domain, and a deal believed to be worth £5 million initially was finally completed midway through the window.

Denmark Under-19 international goalkeeper Daniel Iversen would soon follow Amartey from Scandinavia to Leicester. In medieval times the Danes came to conquer Leicester but with Kasper Schmeichel also on City's books, the Danes were much more welcome these days. Impressive teenage full-back Ben Chilwell also signed a new contract as the club's transfer window strategy seemed to be more about the long-term future rather than the squad's immediate deficiencies.

Ranieri was being asked about transfer business constantly and at one stage he declared there would be no more business: City were done. It may have been an attempt to stop the questions, and the speculation, but it didn't work. It wasn't accurate either. City were linked with a host of players, some with a basis of truth and some that were pure fantasy. Former Manchester City midfielder Nigel de Jong and Roma legend Francesco Totti fell into the latter category.

City had expressed an interest previously in Sporting Lisbon winger André Carrillo, with reports in the summer stating that the club had had a bid of around £9.5 million rejected. The president of the Portuguese club, Bruno de Carvalho, was less than complimentary then about contract rebel Carrillo – and about City. 'The only proposal that I received was that of Leicester,' he was quoted as saying by the Portuguese media, adding sarcastically: 'Is Carrillo good or not? If he is good, why has the only proposal been that of Leicester, this colossus of world football?' No surprise then that City's interest in Carrillo didn't appear to have been followed up, and although there was interest in Sampdoria's highly rated 17-year-old defender Pedro Pereira, no deal was forthcoming there either.

There was plenty of speculation over the future of Gökhan Inler. The Switzerland captain had been signed as replacement for Esteban Cambiasso, but he had struggled to break into the side, much to the frustration of all parties. With Switzerland qualifying for the European Championships, it was important for Inler to gain some game time if he was to lead his country in France, and that led to attempts by some clubs to sign him on loan. Aston Villa wanted Inler, and Schalke manager André Breitenreiter confirmed he had tried to sign him too, but Breitenreiter said he wasn't convinced Inler wanted to leave City. He was right: Inler wanted to stay and fight for his place, gambling on his international future in a bid to crack the Premier League.

Andrej Kramarić had also found himself out in the cold. Kramarić had signed for City just a year before in a deal that was potentially worth over £9 million but had featured just twice in the league, both times as a substitute. It was no surprise when he joined Bundesliga club Hoffenheim on loan for the rest of the campaign, while Yohan Benalouane was also on his way, to Fiorentina on loan, just a few months after joining City.

As a result of Kramarić's departure, it was clear City would be in the hunt for a new striker and would be trying to land one before the close of play on transfer deadline night. Two candidates soon emerged as the front-runners: Sampdoria striker Éder and CSKA Moscow striker Ahmed Musa. City would go toe to toe with Italian giants Inter Milan for Éder. Inter had the prestigious name and reputation, but City were armed with the financial muscle of the club's owners and the chance to play in the Premier League. In the end, despite reports City had a £10 million offer accepted by Sampdoria, prestige won out as Éder opted for the status of Inter, although having City involved in such a bidding war for his services meant he came out of it with a better personal package from Inter than otherwise would have been the case.

City had already had a £15 million bid for Nigeria international Musa rejected. The improved financial status of Russian football had meant they could now compete with Premier League clubs and they were reluctant to part with their main striker. City were reportedly quoted a hugely inflated £23 million asking price and that was the end of that.

So, it came to transfer deadline night and City were no closer to landing a new striker. There was interest in AC Milan striker M'Baye Niang, but City decided not to follow that interest up, while Chelsea striker Loïc Rémy had emerged as an option. Rémy had been on City's radar throughout the window and as their preferred targets failed to materialise he became a more attractive option.

Rémy had scored against City at the King Power Stadium earlier in the season but had struggled to break into the Chelsea starting line-up, despite their struggles. City would attempt to bring him in before the 11pm deadline. Stoke City striker Mame Biram Diouf also became a possibility during the afternoon but City didn't take up the option and so all their eggs were in the Rémy basket. A loan deal until the end of the season seemed the most likely arrangement and as the clock ticked down it looked as though it would happen, as the player was said to be interested, while Chelsea were open to the idea – until they suddenly pulled the plug.

Transfer deals close to deadlines are lined up like a stack of dominoes, with deals dependent in many cases on others being done. It is only once one or two of the dominoes start to fall that others tumble too. This was the case with the Rémy deal: Chelsea decided to hang on to the Frenchman as cover because there was a chance Colombian Radamel Falcao, on loan from Monaco, could be on his way to China. In the end that deal didn't happen either but nevertheless City were left with three frontline strikers for the remainder of the season.

It wasn't for the want of trying by the club but many City supporters were left frustrated that a big-name striker hadn't arrived. However, any disappointment was certainly negated by the fact that City had kept their big hitters for the big push.

JANUARY SUMMARY

Competition	Date	Fixture
Premier League	Sat 2 Jan	Leicester 0-0 Bournemouth
FA Cup – Third Round	Sun 10 Jan	Tottenham 2-2 Leicester
Premier League	Wed 13 Jan	Tottenham 0-1 Leicester
Premier League	Sat 16 Jan	Aston Villa 1-1 Leicester
FA Cup – Third Round	Wed 20 Jan	Leicester 0-2 Tottenham
Premier League	Sat 23 Jan	Leicester 3-0 Stoke

*By the end of January, City had opened up
a three-point lead at the top of the league:*

*25-1 – 2 January (after drawing at home with Bournemouth,
having also drawn with Man City on 29 December)*

10-1 – 14 January (the day after winning at Tottenham)

*8-1 – 24 January (after Arsenal lost at home to Chelsea,
and the day after Leicester beat Stoke at home and
Manchester City drew against West Ham)*

FEBRUARY 2016

		P	W	D	L	GF	GA	GD	Pts
1	Leicester City	23	13	8	2	42	26	16	47
2	Manchester City	23	13	5	5	45	23	22	44
3	Arsenal	23	13	5	5	37	22	15	44
4	Tottenham Hotspur	23	11	9	3	41	19	22	42

Standings on 1 February

City have many club mottos. Above the tunnel at the King Power Stadium is the slogan 'Foxes Never Quit', an attitude they had displayed on a regular basis earlier in the season. However, the club had adopted another slogan, one for the modern, social media era: #Fearless. That was certainly apt now as City displayed no apprehension ahead of the tricky trio of fixtures.

Still, despite their status as the league leaders, City were not the favourites for the title. Manchester City were still favoured by the bookmakers, with Arsenal second and City tied at 8-1 with Tottenham Hotspur in third. That was probably the way Ranieri and City wanted it.

Nonetheless, on home soil City were now being made favourites to beat every side, even against a club like Liverpool which had dominated English football in the 1980s and were the most decorated English team in Europe. That was in the past. This was City's and Jamie Vardy's time.

Vardy was set to put pen to paper on a new, bumper contract when City took on Liverpool at the King Power Stadium, and he justified the investment by the club with a stunning strike as City clinched another 2-0 win.

Vardy had developed a reputation for instinctive finishing inside the penalty area, but racing into space behind defences and beating the keeper was his trademark. Strikes from outside the box just weren't in his repertoire. Or so it was believed. Yet in the second half he latched on to Mahrez's pass in behind the Liverpool defence and instead of turning on the afterburners and going for goal, Vardy shocked everyone, including Reds keeper Simon Mignolet, who was off his line and scrambling back towards goal, by allowing the ball to bounce once before smashing an exquisite volley over the head of Mignolet from 30 yards out.

It was a goal that had everyone jumping to their feet in

amazement. Even the press pack, which is supposed to be devoid of emotional reactions to goals, leapt up in astonishment at what they had just seen. You can adopt a professional demeanour as much as you want as a sports writer but occasionally moments of such brilliance, of such soul-soaring skill arrive that stir even the most hardened of hacks. This was one of them.

BBC Radio Leicester commentator Ian Stringer is renowned for his zealous, throat-bursting reactions to City goals, but this was the one time when even his colourful reaction didn't quite do Vardy's strike justice for his listeners. It was probably impossible to do so. There was no vocal register high enough.

It was Vardy's magical moment. That goal was to be replayed on television constantly for days. The fact he scored City's second too went largely forgotten, but he took his tally to 18 for the season by latching on to Okazaki's deflected shot to rifle the ball into the top corner from six yards out. It was a Vardy bread-and-butter goal, but all talk afterwards was about his stunning first.

'It was unbelievable what Vardy did,' said Ranieri. 'He watched the ball arrive, watched the opponent and watched the goalkeeper. He saw him out of the goal and shot; it was amazing, unbelievable, fantastic.' The Italian even compared Vardy to Holland legend Marco van Basten, who famously scored an astonishing volley in the Euro 88 final against the Soviet Union.

Against Liverpool, City had faced a side at the beginning of their journey under a new manager, Jürgen Klopp. Against Manchester City they were facing the end of an era. Manuel Pellegrini, the Citizens' manager, had dropped a bombshell in a press conference a few days earlier that he was leaving. Everyone in the media suite at the King Power

Stadium had watched the television screens avidly as he finished the conference by stating he would be moving on at
the end of the season. Shortly after, the club announced
that Pep Guardiola, the current Bayern Munich and former
Barcelona manager, would be taking over.

The timing of the news seemed odd. Pellegrini had made
his announcement so matter-of-factly, just as the journalists
expected him to stand up and leave the room, and then the
announcement on Guardiola followed so quickly after that
it had to be planned. Or was it? Either way a reaction from
the Manchester City players was expected. It was just a case
of whether it was a positive or negative one. Leicester's visit
to the Etihad Stadium would be the first home game for the
Citizens since Pellegrini's announcement. Would it galvanise
his players? Or would the Foxes suffer a backlash from a
talented side that had been so obviously underperforming?

To celebrate the Chinese year of the monkey, there were
live primates outside the Etihad Stadium when Leicester fans
arrived at the Etihad. Ranieri's men would end up making
monkeys out of the title favourites.

If ever there was an illustration of the financial gulf
that exists in English football, it is the comparison between
Manchester City and Leicester City. Leicester are not a poor
club by any stretch of the imagination, but what the Citizens
have been able to produce with the finances of the Abu
Dhabi Group eclipses everything else in English football.

Situated in Beswick, Greater Manchester, the Etihad
Stadium is more than just a football ground. It is a futuristic oasis in a working-class inner-city suburb of Manchester.
Maine Road was the club's former ground and that was
extremely traditional in design and feel. Many Manchester
City fans may have lamented the loss of their spiritual
home, but the Etihad is on another level. It isn't just one

stadium. The Citizens' youth teams and under-21s have their own grounds, while even the Asda across the road is state-of-the-art architecture, all gleaming, polished metal.

Traffic problems on the notoriously bad M6 meant many Leicester fans missed the start of the game, and by the time they were able to enter the ground their team were already 1-0 up. Robert Huth had taken advantage of some terrible marking to convert Riyad Mahrez's free-kick after just three minutes. But it would get even better for the Foxes.

At the start of the second half Leicester broke quickly and Kanté played Mahrez into space. The Algerian still had plenty to do but he beat £30 million defender Nicolas Otamendi with a deft touch and then bamboozled his Argentinian central defensive partner Martín Demichelis with a delicious lollipop before sending goalkeeper Joe Hart the wrong way. It was a very different goal to Vardy's against Liverpool but it was just as impressive. It was another breathtaking moment of skill in what was becoming a catalogue of them. Were these really City players who possessed this astonishing ability?

It wasn't just at the attacking end of the pitch where City were displaying world-class form. Kasper Schmeichel pulled off a wonderful save to deny substitute Fernando Reges shortly after. But overall it was still Leicester who were in the ascendency and Huth scored his second of the game with a thumping header from Christian Fuchs's corner, making Sergio Agüero's late strike a mere consolation for the hosts.

Around 60,000 people were packed inside the Etihad Stadium but Leicester had stunned them into silence, while at the same time announcing boldly they were serious title contenders. The home fans sportingly acknowledged that their team had simply been beaten by the better side by applauding the Leicester players as they left the pitch. It had been billed as the showdown between the two title rivals pre-match but the Foxes convincingly beat Pellegrini's men on their own turf to move five points clear at the top of the table.

It was a win that seemed to finally convince many that Leicester's title challenge was very real, and the bookmakers instantly installed the Foxes as favourites to lift the Premier League trophy afterwards. If City fans didn't think it could get any better, it was announced just a few hours later that Vardy had signed his new contract. The perfect end to a near-perfect day. Even the M6 behaved itself for the drive home.

Everyone was talking about Leicester and their incredible emergence as genuine title contenders, but Ranieri was quick to deflect any pressure elsewhere. 'The pressure was on us at the beginning because our goal was to maintain our Premier League status,' he said, 'but now the pressure is on the other teams who spent a lot of money to win the Premier League and Champions League. Now we just enjoy.'

Ranieri was certainly enjoying himself. He would later reveal that he had placed a wager with his players, offering them a whole week off if they could pick up a maximum nine points from the games against Liverpool, Manchester City and the upcoming trip to Arsenal. Two down, one to go.

LEICESTER MERCURY BLOG, 10 FEBRUARY 2016
A TRIP TO MANCHESTER

Five hours.

That is how long it took me to drive (there wasn't a lot of driving going on) the 100 miles or so up the M6 to the Etihad Stadium.

But despite arriving 20 minutes into the game, having

missed the start of a fixture for the first time in my career, and Robert Huth's opening goal, what I witnessed once I was eventually in the ground made it all worthwhile.

It was an outstanding display by Leicester City.

This was no smash and grab raid, Leicester were worthy winners and dismantled Manchester City in the second half, having soaked up a lot of pressure in the first half.

The final score was 3-1 but that flattered Man City, as Leicester created several other good opportunities to score more.

It was a performance and result that has finally started to earn Leicester the credit they deserve.

Finally, it seems people around the game are taking City seriously.

And that is why it could start to get tricky for the Foxes from now on.

Judging by what I saw, I don't think Manuel Pellegrini's men truly took Leicester seriously, but now I think Arsenal will this Sunday.

Man City looked like a side that thought they would easily roll Leicester over and expose them for the upstarts that they are.

For all the millions spent and all the undeniable talent they possess, Man City simply didn't match Ranieri's men for the fundamentals; work rate, desire and hunger. Three basic ingredients for any successful side.

People are trying to find the secret to Leicester's transformation, the reasons why they have managed to shatter the established perceptions of how a Premier League season should go.

Logic would suggest that City, a side that was bottom of the table for such a large part of last season, should not be where they are, or anywhere near where they are.

But they are defying logic through sheer bloody-mindedness.

Leicester wanted the win more than the previous title favourites. They worked harder, ran further, threw their bodies in to make blocks and protect their goal, and when the key moments came at both ends of the field they had the quality to make the most of them.

It wasn't just Robert Huth's physicality at set pieces or Riyad Mahrez's sublime skill to beat two defenders who have cost £35 million combined to score a superb second goal for Ranieri's men, it was also Kasper Schmeichel's incredible reflex save to deny Fernando Reges in the second half.

But Leicester's hunger is one of the biggest factors in their success and it only takes a closer look at each player's back-story to understand where it comes from.

So many of the starting line-up have either faced rejection or overcome adversity in their career.

Kasper Schmeichel: Had to cope with living in the shadow of his famous father and was surprisingly allowed to leave Leeds United with Simon Grayson saying he wasn't good enough.

Danny Simpson: Sold by Queens Park Rangers without explanation, and to his own surprise, having helped them to promotion to the Premier League.

Robert Huth: Sold by Chelsea and then unwanted by Stoke City.

Marc Albrighton: Released by Aston Villa, the club he had been with since the age of eight.

Danny Drinkwater: Schooled by Manchester United but farmed out repeatedly on loan and then sold to City.

Riyad Mahrez: Learned to play football on the streets of Paris, not in an academy, and didn't sign a professional contract until he was 19, having been told initially he was too small.

N'Golo Kanté: Another who was told he was too small and not good enough in possession when he was emerging.

Jamie Vardy: Again, told he was too small when released by Sheffield Wednesday and had to fight his way through the non-league ranks to return to the professional game.

The upshot is you have a group of players who all feel they have something to prove and a manager who knows how to channel that desire in the right way.

They will need that character because, as I said previously, City's win at Manchester City will mean things will get tougher from here on in.

Teams will know that to stand any chance of stopping Leicester they are going to have to match them yard for yard, tackle for tackle, block for block. That will physically test them.

The question is can they match Leicester's hunger, and that is purely a mental matter.

Suddenly, everyone was taking City seriously, including their title rivals. Despite the bookmakers' odds making them favourites, the weight of expectation was still on Manchester City and Arsenal, and even Tottenham.

The Gunners fans had been waiting 12 years for another Premier League title and for many it had been too long. If

it wasn't Manchester United beating them to the punch it
was Chelsea, and now in recent seasons Manchester City had
emerged as well to scupper their plans. Now, with Chelsea
and United completely out of sorts, and Manchester City suffering their own problems, there was the sense that Arsenal
wouldn't have a better opportunity. If Wenger couldn't win
the title this season with his usual rivals experiencing such
a poor campaign, when would they? Leicester's emergence
had really put a spanner in the works and heaped more pressure on Wenger, who was the subject of calls to step down by
some Arsenal fans. Wenger would do his best to deflect some
of that pressure on to Ranieri.

'In one week, Leicester have beaten Liverpool and
Manchester City, so that means that they suddenly become
the favourite to win the Premier League,' said Wenger, ahead
of Leicester's visit to north London. 'We have a big game at
home now against Leicester, and I believe we have enough
quality and nerves to deal with that. We have been in a title
race and we are still in it.

'Leicester is a fantastic example that football is not
only about just spending the money. Of course [the whole
country wants City to win], and it's natural. It's normal. The
advantage they have until the end of the season: apart from
our fans and the [Manchester] City fans and Tottenham fans,
the rest of the country is behind Leicester.'

'You reproach me about not buying big names,' he
added, 'but you will support the team who has no big names!'

The Emirates Stadium. Another sprawling, enormous,
futuristic ground which seems out of place among the rows
of north London terraced houses that surround it. Like an
alien spaceship that has landed in the middle of suburbia,
it dominates the landscape but doesn't seem to fit in with
it. Such stadia are the future of the game, with attendances

soaring, and progress can't be stopped; but just like when City left Filbert Street to move to their new stadium in 2002, one sometimes feels that a part of Arsenal's soul was left behind at their traditional former ground, Highbury.

There was a sense that this was a game Arsenal simply had to win. All the pressure was on Wenger, and that pressure increased dramatically as City took the lead through Jamie Vardy's penalty just before half-time. Nacho Monreal clumsily stuck out a leg and turned his back on Vardy, who made sure there was plenty of contact to convince referee Martin Atkinson it was a penalty. There were those who disputed the decision, stating that Vardy had run into Monreal, but it was poor defending from the Arsenal full-back and deserved punishment. Monreal committed the same mistake on Mahrez at the start of the second half but got away with it as Atkinson waved away Mahrez's appeals.

The game was going exactly to plan. City had soaked up pressure and got their noses in front so, just like Manchester City the week before, the Gunners now had to come out more at City, leaving them susceptible to the counter-attack. However, Danny Simpson was then sent off for two bookable offences inside five minutes and it proved to be the turning point as goals from substitutes Theo Walcott and then Danny Welbeck, with literally the last touch of the game, gave Arsenal the victory. City's lead at the top of the table was cut to just two points.

Again, City felt aggrieved at the dismissal as they appeared to be 'soft' fouls by Simpson. But once they were a man light, City struggled to maintain their high-octane, pressing game as there were now too many gaps to cover and the Gunners' pressure told in the end. The Emirates erupted at the final whistle and the Arsenal players celebrated a potentially crucial victory. It looked almost like the end of a cup final. The Gunners players would post selfies of themselves celebrating the win in the dressing room – but ultimately they would be unable to capitalise on their victory.

LEICESTER MERCURY BLOG, 19 FEBRUARY 2016
RAZZMATAZZ

The whole world has fallen in love with Leicester City.

I know that is a bold statement that can't possibly be quantified, but that is how it has felt over the past couple of weeks.

Even before City's incredible win at Manchester City there was an endless stream of overseas film crews, radio stations and journalists contacting the *Mercury* for comment on the remarkable story that is City's season.

It has gone beyond the stage of 'Who are Leicester City?' It has also taken a step further than just 'How is this possible?'

Now the big question that is coming thick and fast is 'Can they do it? Can they become Premier League champions?'

Following the win at the Etihad Stadium, the media interest from abroad moved up another notch. It moved from a mild interest, a fleeting curiosity in what may have been perceived to be a temporary glitch in the established order of the Premier League, to a ravenous media hunger, an insatiable appetite for anything to do with City.

Heaven knows what it must have been like for the club, but from a personal point of view the phone calls, emails and tweets have become relentless.

I have been interviewed for radio shows from America, Australia, New Zealand and Canada, as well as our own national radio stations. I even had a call one Sunday night from BBC 5Live asking me to record a 90-second spot that was run the next morning detailing the five key games City will face over the coming weeks.

It was a little disconcerting the next day in the office when colleagues said they had been awoken by my Brummie tones wafting through their bedside radios. Like Peter Kay's Chorley FM catchphrase, I was coming in their ears!

But that was only the start. Last Thursday was my day off, but it started with a trip into the office to film a brief spot for a Norwegian television station before I drove down to the Premier League Production Studios in Hertfordshire to film a 90-minute live television show, stopping at Watford Gap Services en route to take a call from an Aussie radio station.

When I arrived at PLP, I was ushered into a Green Room, which wasn't green by the way. My fellow guest was national sports writer Steve Bates, a veteran of the *Sunday Supplement*, who was taking everything in his stride, unlike me.

On arrival, I was asked what I wanted to drink and to eat, and I could have anything I liked, within reason. I wasn't used to this and didn't confess to the homemade sandwich I had left in the car. Make hay while the sun shines, I say. 'A ham and cheese toastie please?' Let the good times roll!

Lobster Thermidor may have been taking the Michael.

Then it was through to make-up, an experience I wasn't used to. It was simply to cover up any blemishes or shiny spots, but I did notice the make-up lady spent a considerable time dusting my bald head with a sponge. In fact, this would be a regular occurrence that afternoon.

Then it was into the studio where Mark Pougatch was hosting the show, which I discovered was going live to 120 countries outside Europe. Hello Tanzania.

It was a similar set-up to *Match of the Day*, where Gary

Lineker sits opposite two guests and asks their opinions on that weekend's events, only on this occasion the entire first 30 minutes was devoted to Leicester City.

Having been an avid viewer of *Match of the Day* for years, it was fascinating to see it from the other side of the camera. The room was deathly quiet and the cameras seem to float around the room, undetected. Prompters with the script for Mark to read were set at various points within his eye line, so it would seem he was effortlessly and casually talking to the viewer.

There was a monitor set in the coffee table just in front of us so we could see all the footage or visuals that were being referred to, although viewers couldn't see it.

I tried to impart my knowledge about Leicester City with conviction and authority, but only occasionally did I say anything they didn't know.

'They found Riyad Mahrez by accident you know!' That caused a few raised eyebrows.

'Who were they watching?'

'Mendes, who is now at Forest.'

'Really?'

There were several advertising breaks, which were filled with more dusting of my bald head, and then we were done.

But I wasn't.

On Sunday, US news channel CNN, which I had spoken to a couple of times on the phone, asked me to head down to their offices just off Regent Street.

Following filing my copy after City's controversial defeat at the Emirates Stadium, I headed down to Oxford Circus for this interview.

After walking out of the subway I immediately noticed that the London Palladium, which was significantly smaller than I ever imagined, was hosting the auditions for *Britain's Got Talent* just around the corner from the CNN offices.

There was a huge Bentley parked outside with security all around it, so I assumed that was Simon Cowell's ride.

I was taken inside CNN and again invited into a Green Room, which again wasn't green.

After ten minutes, I was asked to enter a small room and was told to stare at a black monitor displaying a broken horizontal white line – it was rather like looking into a black hole! I had to pretend that the broken line was the person I was talking to and was told to stare at it throughout the interview. As a distraction, there was a monitor just below this with the actual footage of the person asking the questions from Atlanta, Georgia, and the visual of me positioned next to it.

With an earpiece in, I could hear everything being asked, although the temptation was always there to look down. It was like fighting acrophobia. Whatever you do, don't look down!

It lasted just five minutes, during which time I blinked incessantly – as my nine-year-old niece was quick to point out to me the next day.

Interview finished, I found myself back on the streets of London, only to have to quickly sidestep a dance troupe who appeared to be dressed as Roman soldiers, running barefoot down the pavement outside the Palladium.

They were quickly followed by a group of girls in tartan, who were also whooping and smiling, almost in complete disbelief, so I assume they both got through.

But I guess that is how most City fans feel at the moment, in complete amazement at this remarkable story which has put little old Leicester City in the consciousness of people around the world.

Talk about Britain having talent!

City's defeat to the Gunners at the King Power Stadium earlier in the season had been a pivotal moment in City's season. Their naivety had been exposed. They had been picked apart by a team more street savvy and skilled than them. There had been a philosophical reaction to that defeat, a sense that City had to learn from it and adapt. They had done just that and had arrived at the Emirates all grown up. However, the manner of the defeat, the last-gasp Welbeck winner and the controversy of the Simpson sending-off had left a bitter taste in the mouth.

It is at times like this that clubs look to an experienced, level-headed player and an authoritative figure to handle the media. Normally, it is the captain Wes Morgan who takes on the responsibility, but goalkeeper Kasper Schmeichel, the vice-captain, handles those moments better than most. Schmeichel has had a lot to contend with in his career. The son of Manchester United's legendary goalkeeper Peter Schmeichel, the Dane has had to put up with comparisons from the moment he first donned a pair of gloves. While it may have been a help, as he has obviously inherited his father's ability and had been around football from the moment he could walk, it has also been a cross to bear. Kasper is constantly asked about being the son of Peter to the extent that now he just shrugs his shoulders and yawns. The first time I met him to interview him, he set me a challenge: 'I bet you can't write about me without mentioning my father!' I tried, I really did, but at times I have failed. He is bored by the comparisons, but there are obvious ones, besides the fact he is also a keeper and has the same blond hair. He makes himself look as large as possible in the same trademark fashion as his dad when strikers are bearing down on goal, and he has raced forwards in the same way as Peter to join the attack at set-pieces in the dying seconds of games when City have been chasing an equaliser or winner. Against Yeovil Town during the Championship title-winning season, his header in added time seemed to cross the line before bouncing out but Chris Wood made sure of the equaliser from close range and the goal was eventually confirmed to have been given to Wood.

Schmeichel Senior has stated in the past how he felt his surname and the weight of expectation associated with it have been something of a hindrance to his son. He felt Kasper wouldn't have had to drop down to the lower leagues to get his career up and running, that he would have had more opportunities earlier in his career, without the burden of being a Schmeichel.

However, it should be noted that Kasper, who had been a striker earlier in his youth before choosing to be a keeper as he felt he could progress faster, had sprung to prominence as a 15-year-old when he came on as a substitute in a charity game to mark the anniversary of Denmark's 1992 European Championship win, a game involving his father, who had played in Denmark's moment of triumph. The reserve keeper hadn't been available to replace Peter, who played the second half in attack, so Kasper was called upon. After making a string of saves, he was asked to train with Brøndby, his father's first club. After impressing at an international tournament, he was then signed by Manchester City at the age of 16.

Kasper had come through the ranks at Manchester City on schoolboy and scholar terms before turning professional. He had gone out on loan to Darlington, Bury, Falkirk, Cardiff City and Coventry City, but he found his route to the first team at the Etihad Stadium blocked and he dropped down to League Two to rejoin former Citizens manager Sven-Göran Eriksson at Notts County. Eriksson would also sign him for Leicester in June 2011, from Leeds United, in what was a strange transfer saga.

Normally in England, transfer deals are done quietly without public comment by either club, but in this case Leeds chose to announce they had accepted an offer of £1.25 million from Leicester for Schmeichel. Shortly afterwards, the then Leeds boss (and former Leicester City captain) Simon Grayson issued a statement saying the Yorkshire club felt it would be difficult to agree a new contract with Schmeichel, who had only a year left on his current agreement and denied on Twitter that he had been offered a new one. Grayson even suggested the move would help shore up his defence. 'When you concede the number of goals that we did, it's obviously an area where one or two players are vulnerable and we need to change it around slightly,' he said. 'There are good options for goalkeepers and defenders out there, so this was a footballing decision first and foremost. When Kasper goes we have other alternatives that will make us better and keep progressing us. I have spoken to him to explain my decision. If no bid had come, it wouldn't have changed the position that we were looking for another goalkeeper and it would be highlighted even more.'

Schmeichel had only found out about the deal, he would later explain, when a friend called him to wish him luck at Leicester. He was shocked, but he was also probably driven to be an even bigger success at City by Grayson's inference that he hadn't been good enough for Leeds.

In his first season at Leicester Schmeichel was named the club's player of the year and the players' player of the year, and since then he has gone from strength to strength. City have a proud history of having great goalkeepers. England's World Cup-winning goalkeeper of 1966, Gordon Banks, started at Leicester and he was eventually replaced by Peter Shilton, who became England's most capped player ever. Schmeichel has ensured over the past few seasons that he will be mentioned alongside those greats by City fans when they discuss the club's greatest players in the pubs and cafés of the city.

'It has been an incredible ride for him considering his background,' teammate and fellow goalkeeper Mark Schwarzer said in an interview with Talksport. 'Everyone talks about his dad, the great Peter Schmeichel, and he truly was. He revolutionised goalkeeping. He was the best goalkeeper on the planet for a number of years. Kasper had to grow up with that and then wanted to take the same path and become a goalkeeper. It must have been difficult for him but he has done remarkably well and is maturing. He is at the right age now, and he is getting better and better all the time, and this season particularly he has played very well and proved any critics wrong.'

He had become City's Mr Reliable as the last line of defence, and when they needed a cool head in front of the media, he did that job as well.

LEICESTER MERCURY BLOG, 23 FEBRUARY 2016
HAPPY-GO-LUCKY

People are forever striving for their lost youth.

Whether it is cosmetic surgery, special creams and lotions or a special diet, people are constantly searching for something that will make them feel young again.

Well, I think I have found the answer, Leicester City's own elixir of youth, if you will.

If you are a football fan and you want to feel that youthful buzz of your adolescence then just watch N'Golo Kanté play football.

I am not talking about his appearance, which away from the pitch always seems to be of a happy-go-lucky schoolboy who is in awe of everything around him, smiling incessantly as if the school holidays had just started.

Between Kanté and Shinji Okazaki, it is hard to predict which of them would win an award for being the happiest, smiliest person down the training ground. It certainly wouldn't be Club Ambassador Alan 'The Birch' Birchenall.

He has a wide-eyed innocence about him which is very endearing. I bet there are elderly ladies all over Leicester who just want to hug him and plant a smacker on his cherub cheeks before giving him 20p for pocket money to buy some Black Jacks and Fruit Salads, or even a Curly Wurly, although like everything from my childhood they aren't as big as they used to be.

However, on the pitch Kanté is a breath of fresh air, a player who looks like he plays for the sheer love of the game, free from pressure, nerves or fear.

It doesn't look like it would matter whether he was playing in front of 60,000 or six people. Nothing seems to faze him.

In an interview with the City media staff he said his style of play was developed while playing on the streets or down the park with his mates in Paris. It looks like it too. You can tell.

I don't think I have ever seen a player who works so hard and is full of so much enthusiasm.

People talk about his ability to win the ball back, how he leads the stats for ball recovery and how it seems at times like he has more than two legs, or even telescopic legs as he always, somehow, seems to come away with the ball.

It is an impressive skill. As he showed at Arsenal, he may give the ball away from time to time but you don't have to wait too long for him to win it back, and they are nearly all clean tackles as well. For someone who makes the amount of challenges he does he very rarely gives free kicks away. It's like playing football with an eager puppy that gets between your legs and always ends up coming away with the ball.

With the ball he is equally impressive. When in possession he wastes no time – he isn't frozen by doubt or a lack of confidence. It seems almost instinctive to just start running with the ball, bursting towards the defenders before him at pace, looking to commit them.

In his mind I wonder if he sees the white posts and the net beyond them or a couple of jumpers rolled up and chucked to the ground.

We have all watched players who look as though they would rather be somewhere else. Football is a profession and to some it is just that, a job. It is something to do to pay the bills.

Kanté is different. He doesn't play to live, he lives to play.

THE EARTH TREMBLES AS
THE TITLE RACE HOTS UP

The players had lost their bet with Claudio Ranieri.

The wager had been a full week off if they could pick up a full set of nine points from the three games against Liverpool, Manchester City and Arsenal. They had come up short at the Emirates Stadium in controversial fashion but

Ranieri decided their efforts warranted an extended break. It was another master stroke of man-management.

'I gave them the week off because they deserve it,' said Ranieri. 'They did a magnificent performance and I am very proud of them, so I give to them the week off. I have never done this before in my career.'

The players flew off to various destinations to recharge their batteries, while Ranieri returned to Rome. Jamie Vardy would later state that it was a crucial decision: 'It was a great idea; I went to Dubai and I remember sitting on a sun lounger and in the same hotel, Sunderland were there running up and down the beach doing fitness. For me to be relaxing while they were doing their training was quite nice. It worked out perfectly. No one was going to go on a seven-day bender. We were there to relax with family and that's all we did until we got back to training.'

Some pundits said it was a mistake, that City should have got straight back on to the training pitch after the Arsenal defeat to prepare for the next game, the home clash with Norwich City, but Ranieri knew his side needed to be physically ready for a run of five fixtures before the next international break that he felt could make or break their season. After the visit of the Canaries, City were to entertain West Bromwich Albion, then travel to Watford, then take on Newcastle United at the King Power Stadium before heading back to London to play Crystal Palace.

'There are five matches now – I believe this could be our season if we get through these five battles,' said Ranieri. 'I think we are at the turn, then the run-in and the goal is there. I think this is the key moment for us.'

Just as they had after the first defeat to Arsenal, City had the chance to bounce back against the Canaries, and they took it, but it was a nervy afternoon. Were it not for some poor finishing from Norwich, particularly Cameron Jerome, Ranieri's decision to give the players a week off would have come under even more scrutiny. But in contrast to the late, late heartache at Arsenal in the previous game, it was last-minute joy against Norwich as substitute Leonardo Ulloa popped up with an 89th-minute winner. The relief was palpable – and the King Power Stadium erupted to such an extent the celebrations caused an earthquake.

Geology students from the University of Leicester and scientists had installed a seismometer at a nearby school, 500 metres away from the ground, and as Ulloa's goal hit the back of the net and the Blue Army, all 30,000 of them, jumped to their feet, there was a tremor recording 0.3 on the Richter Scale.

It was also another significant contribution from Ulloa. The Argentinian had endured a frustrating campaign from a personal point of view. Only twice had he started back-to-back games all season as Shinji Okazaki had slowly established himself as Ranieri's preferred partner for Jamie Vardy. The previous season Ulloa had finished as City's top scorer, but now he was playing a supporting role. However, his attitude epitomised the spirit within the squad. At other clubs, players who were once first choice but were now coming off the substitute's bench regularly could be expected to sulk, but not Ulloa, nor the other City squad members. The key to City's success had been that everyone knew their role, whether it was starting and coming off after 70 minutes like Okazaki every week, or Ulloa coming on for the last 20, and everyone had been fully committed when called upon. They all had character and desire to be successful.

Ulloa's story is a remarkable one, a tale of sacrifice as he left his family behind to try to make his fortune playing football. Anyone who has listened to Ulloa talk about his family knows how difficult a decision that must have been.

He left his home in Argentina at the age of 15 after he was spotted playing for his local club General Roca, in his home city in the north-east of Rio Negro in northern Patagonia, and offered a trial with Primera B Nacional side Comisión de Actividades Infantiles. It was supposed to be a week-long trial but Ulloa ended up staying, living away from his family, studying and training with his new club.

He was picked for Argentina Under-17s and was then signed by San Lorenzo in Buenos Aires. It was tough for Ulloa, being so far away from home, but it was also tough for his family, particularly his mother. 'My mother suffered a lot,' says Ulloa, the youngest of three brothers. 'My father and brothers like football and they knew it was my dream. They suffered but they did not want to stand in my way.'

He stayed 600 miles from home in the Argentine capital, playing for Arsenal de Sarandí and then Olimpo, before he was taken even further away from home, to Europe, to play for Castellón in the Spanish Second Division.

By now he had a wife and a daughter, who were also leaving behind family, but it was a move Ulloa felt he had to make for the sake of his career and he was soon signed by Almería in La Liga. He was top scorer in his first season, with seven goals, but Almería were relegated. However, after scoring 28 the following season he was signed by Brighton and Hove Albion; he would be playing in the Championship.

At the end of the 2012/13 season, City had just been promoted to the Premier League and manager Nigel Pearson was looking for a new striker. He pulled his defenders to one side and asked them who had been the most difficult striker they had faced that season. They all said Ulloa and

City made their move, signing Ulloa for a club record of initially £8 million, rising to £10 million.

Now Ulloa was in the Premier League and his decision to leave home 13 years before had finally paid off. 'Looking back now, they know it was worth it because they see that I achieved my dream,' he says. 'It was hard but all the suffering is forgotten. It was worth it.'

His family are never far from his thoughts, or his skin. On his forearm he has the names of his daughters, Sofia and Morena, tattooed next to a clock face depicting the time of their births, while on his wrist he bears a symbol in honour of his late grandfather, José Omar Ulloa, who died before Ulloa joined City. Because of his commitments to Brighton he couldn't attend the funeral of his beloved grandfather, his 'Abuelo', but he honours him whenever he scores by pointing to the sky, as well as kissing the names of his daughters on his arm.

After his goal against Newcastle United at St James's Park in November, when City picked up a 3-0 win, he had pointed to the sky with both hands, rather than the usual one. Not many people noticed. When no other journalists were around, as he stood on the side of the pitch, I asked him about it. 'The celebration was for my grandmother,' he said. 'She died and she helped me so much when I was growing up so that was all in the celebration after I scored. She died three weeks ago but I feel she helped me all the time and I loved her. It all came out in this moment.'

After his goal against Norwich City, while the earth was still shaking, Ulloa kissed his arm, twice, looked up to the sky and pointed to the heavens.

It wasn't just locally that City were causing tremors; they were sending shockwaves around the world. Amazingly, with just 11 games to go, City were still top of the Premier League, two points clear of Tottenham Hotspur and five ahead of Arsenal. The global media scrutiny was intensifying as the planet was waking up and taking notice of this amazing sporting story. How was it possible, asked many of those who arrived in Leicester to cover City's amazing transformation, that a team that was bottom of the table just a year before could now be leading the Premier League?

People looking for explanations for the sudden and dramatic change in Leicester City's fortunes have examined every possible reason for the team's form. They have looked at the change of manager, the subtle tweak in tactics and the introduction of new players. Many were even starting to believe the Richard III theory. After all, City had now picked up 78 points from 36 games since his reburial.

However, there was another factor to be considered. Marc Albrighton, who had provided the cross for Ulloa's winner against Norwich, was in the City wilderness a year before until his introduction as a half-time substitute in the home win over West Ham United. City then went on to win a further six out of the final eight games to secure survival, with Albrighton an ever-present at wing-back. Albrighton had started every league game since. So, was Albrighton City's lucky talisman?

'It's got to be coincidence,' Albrighton said. 'I'm as modest as they come so I'm not going to say the whole fortunes have changed because of me. I don't see how that would work but it's good for me and in stats it looks good. Since I've come into the team, it has been unbelievable. I think we have only lost three or four games.

'I don't know what it is, but when you're walking off the pitch and the whole stadium is in raptures because you've won again it's fantastic. It is amazing how many good times you can have in a year.'

FEBRUARY SUMMARY

Competition	Date	Fixture
Premier League	Tue 2 Feb	Leicester 2-0 Liverpool
Premier League	Sat 6 Feb	Man City 1-3 Leicester
Premier League	Sun 14 Feb	Arsenal 2-1 Leicester
Premier League	Sat 27 Feb	Leicester 1-0 Norwich

Defeat to Arsenal proved the only blemish on an almost perfect February, the highlight a commanding victory over title rivals Man City:

9-2 – 2 February (after winning at home to Liverpool)

7-4 – 6 February (after winning at Manchester City) –
THE FIRST TIME LEICESTER ARE PRICED AS TITLE FAVOURITES

6-4 – 14 February (after losing at Arsenal; elsewhere,
Manchester City lost at home to Spurs)

MARCH 2016

		P	W	D	L	GF	GA	GD	Pts
1	Leicester City	27	16	8	3	49	29	20	56
2	Tottenham Hotspur	27	15	9	3	49	21	28	54
3	Arsenal	27	15	6	6	43	26	17	51
4	Manchester City	26	14	5	7	48	28	20	47

Standings on 1 March

Ranieri's substitutions against Norwich had proved the Italian was willing to risk all to gain victories, and in the build-up to the visit of West Bromwich Albion he pledged to do exactly the same. City were in it to win it, he said. 'I will take a lot of risks. One point is not enough, we have to win. You can lose but it is one point less. We take the risk and that is why the manager is hired for this reason to take the risk. I enjoy when there is something for me to do. It was okay, it was good because when you make changes and they find the solution it is fantastic.'

However, Ranieri was willing to play the psychological game as well. Sir Alex Ferguson had been a master at taking the pressure off his Manchester United by heaping it on his rivals. When it came to mind games, he had consistently been the winner. Now Ranieri was seeking to do the same.

'Tottenham have been the best team we have played,' said Ranieri. 'Tottenham are strong in every situation, when they defend and when they attack they know very well what they want.

'Everyone is speaking about Leicester but no one is speaking about Tottenham. In my opinion they are the favourites, then Arsenal and Manchester City. I understand we are the surprise, but if we are realistic you say, yes, Leicester have made a fantastic season but the real competitors are Man City, Arsenal and Tottenham.'

Daniel Amartey had made his full debut as Danny Simpson's replacement against Norwich but Simpson returned after his ban to face Albion. N'Golo Kanté was ruled out with a minor hamstring strain, so the ever-reliable Andy King was given the nod by Ranieri to partner Danny Drinkwater in central midfield.

If City had shown how to win when you are not at your best against Norwich, they demonstrated the other side of the coin against Tony Pulis's Albion side. City were outstanding, creating a host of chances, but they were ultimately left frustrated.

City weren't known for being a side that liked to dominate possession. In fact Ranieri would confess his side were at their best when the opposition had the ball. However, on a crisp St David's Day evening it was City who had 65 per cent possession and 22 shots on Albion's goal; but it was Albion who took the lead through Salomón Rondón's 10th-minute goal against the run of play. A deflected strike from Danny Drinkwater and then a superb team goal, rounded off by King, put City in the driving seat, only for Craig Gardner to pinch an equaliser with an excellent free-kick five minutes into the second half and despite plenty of City pressure, there was to be no final flurry, no last-gasp winner, no earthquake this time.

Albion had become the first visitors to score at the King Power Stadium since the turn of the year but Pulis was full of praise for City after the game, standing throughout a brief press conference in which he hardly took a question and simply wanted to praise City.

'We have done brilliant tonight and it is a fantastic point for us but now the game is over I just hope Leicester City win the league,' he said. 'It has been a long time since Nottingham Forest got promoted from the second division to the first and then won the league, and this will be the most surprising shock in the Premier League since then. It would be a bigger shock if they do it because the divide between the Haves and the Have-nots in this league is absolutely enormous. It would be absolutely fantastic for everyone in football if Leicester could do it.

'I am now supporting Leicester City between now and the rest of the season, except for West Bromwich Albion of course. I don't see why they can't do it. If they can keep the enthusiasm up and if they can get the breaks.

'We had some fantastic breaks tonight and defended heroically at times, and we had to. If they get the breaks going their way, because that is what you need at times in football, then just keep going and keep believing. Hopefully they can do it.'

The draw was enough for City to open up a three-point lead at the top of the table.

It was appropriate that it was Wales international King who had scored City's second goal to secure the valuable point. Pundits had dismissed City as title contenders because they said the squad wasn't big or strong enough to sustain a challenge. King had provided another example of the quality Ranieri had at his disposal, and of the selfless attitude of the group.

King had been raised in Maidenhead and joined Chelsea when he was nine years old, but after six years with the club he was released as a 15-year-old in 2004, the year Ranieri was sacked as Chelsea manager. (King had even been a ball boy at Stamford Bridge, sitting just feet away from his future City boss as the Italian stood in the Chelsea technical area.) Although King was disappointed, the negative turned into a positive as City swooped and he finished his football education at Belvoir Drive.

I first interviewed King in 2010 when he was 21 and he has always been mature beyond his years, and a dedicated professional. 'I have always known what I have wanted from a very early age,' he said back then. 'From getting picked up by Chelsea when I was very young, I always thought I was in with a chance of being a professional. Chelsea set that pathway for me, but I am grateful to Leicester for giving me the chance to prove myself. I was at Chelsea from nine to 15 and then I got released. Fortunately, Leicester came in for me and I am so grateful to Jon [Rudkin, head of the academy and now director of football] and Steve [Beaglehole, the Development Squad coach] for giving me the chance to prove myself.

'At the time I was disappointed because I had been with Chelsea a long time. It was just at the start of their [Abramovich] takeover regime and I think a lot of the lads were in a similar position to me. I was fortunate enough to come to Leicester and get more good coaching.

'I have been well looked after at Leicester by all the staff and I am thankful to them for how I have progressed. I like to think I am quite level-headed. I try to take just one step at a time, and take everything in my stride.'

King had been blooded into City's first team under Ian Holloway as they battled for survival in the Championship. He was handed his first-team debut, aged 18, in a 0-0 draw against Wolves in October 2007, and he scored his first goal with an impressive 35-yard strike in a 2-1 defeat to Southampton two months later. He made a total of 11 league appearances that season, a campaign which culminated in City being relegated to League One for the first time ever.

He had served City at the lowest point in the club's history, and here he was now, one of the senior members of a City squad that was top of the Premier League and chasing a first-ever English title. He was also an established member of the Wales squad that had qualified for a major international championship finals – Euro 2016 – for the first time since 1958.

Like so many of his City teammates, King had faced rejection and adversity, but turned them into a positive. After experiencing the dark days of League One, King was making sure he made the most of the good times too.

If City went on to claim a first-ever Premier League title, he would become the first player to have won the title in each of the top three divisions with the same club since several members of the Ipswich Town side of the late 1950s and early 1960s. King, City's Mr Dependable, would surely be included in the list of City legends.

'We are enjoying it and why shouldn't we be? If someone had told us at the start of the season we would be in this position, we would have chopped their hand off for it,' he said. 'So, why shouldn't we enjoy it? We are playing well, with freedom, and winning games brings a good feeling around the training ground and the city. We want to make the most of this season.'

The draw against Albion was seen initially as two points dropped. Leicester had a three-point lead at the top of the table, but Spurs could leapfrog them at the top with victory over West Ham United the following evening, while Arsenal were expected to roll over Swansea City at the Emirates. Manchester City, meanwhile, travelled to Liverpool.

It was to be an evening City fans wouldn't forget, even though their team weren't in action, and it felt like another pivotal moment.

ALL BETS ARE OFF AS CITY CLOSE IN

How do you offer odds of 5000-1 in what effectively is a 20-horse race? On the face of it, it seems a ridiculous risk, but the reason the bookmakers were willing to offer such long odds was simply because teams like Leicester City are not supposed to challenge for the Premier League title. They must have thought only the most optimistic, or downright crazy, City fan would throw away even £5 on such an impossible bet.

Now City were three points clear at the top of the table there was a sense of panic among the bookmakers, who began offering those who had taken the odds the opportunity to cash out. Some were looking at winning six-figure sums if City could clinch the title and the bookmakers were estimating they would lose millions.

The *Mercury* began to hear of such punters, who were starting to accept cash-out offers. John Pryke, a 59-year-old dad of three, had placed a £20 bet on a whim at the start of the season and was on course to win £100,000. John, who answered the door to the *Mercury* reporter who tracked him down dressed as Snoopy from Peanuts, for no other reason that he felt like it, eventually cashed in at £29,000. It wasn't a case of the devoted City fan not believing in his team, it was because the huge amount of money he could have won was spoiling his enjoyment of a season he never thought he would ever experience. He wanted to savour it without stressing over what he could potentially win or lose.

He wasn't the only one. An unnamed punter had put £50 on City and was set to win £250,000 but decided to cash out for £72,335. 'Win or lose the league, I'm looking forward to the rest of the season ahead,' said the anonymous City fan. 'It will mean so much if we win, so there's no point in being greedy.'

City fans couldn't lose. If they cashed out they received a life-changing sum of money, and if City went on to win the title they would still be able to enjoy the greatest moment in the history of the club they loved and cherished.

As City headed to Watford for their next game, on 5 March, they knew they had a huge opportunity. Their rivals had failed to take the chance to reel them back in as they had all lost crucial midweek fixtures; furthermore, as the City players travelled to Vicarage Road to face the Hornets in the late kick-off game, Arsenal and Tottenham had played out a thrilling 2-2 draw. City knew they could go five points clear with victory.

Vicarage Road had been the scene of one of City's most heartbreaking moments in recent seasons: 12 May, 2013 – a day City fans will never forget, no matter how much they try. It was the play-off semi-final second leg against Watford. A place at Wembley and the chance to snatch promotion to the Premier League would be the prize for the victors. City had a 1-0 lead from the first leg at the King Power Stadium, courtesy of David Nugent's late winner.

A couple of seasons before City had missed out on a trip to Wembley when they lost a dramatic penalty shoot-out at Cardiff City. The Foxes had had the new Wembley arch in their sights after overturning a first-leg deficit but Frenchman Yann Kermorgant had tried an arrogant chipped penalty, woefully executed, and Leicester left the Cardiff City Stadium in tears. Kermorgant wouldn't play again for City.

Three years later City had had the advantage and Nugent had cancelled Matěj Vydra's early strike to keep the Foxes ahead. Vydra struck again in the second half to level the tie but in the last minute Anthony Knockaert, another Frenchman, earned a penalty that could put City through to Wembley. He stepped up himself. He did nothing wrong but Hornets keeper Manuel Almunia saved his first effort with his legs and then saved the follow-up from Knockaert as well. There wasn't even time for Knockaert to put his head in his hands as Watford broke and within seconds of having the chance to go to the final, Troy Deeney scored at the other end to send City crashing out in the cruellest of late twists.

Watford failed in the final and City had exorcised the demons the following season as they marched to the

Championship title and promotion to the Premier League. Now the Hornets were back in the top flight too and enjoying a strong first campaign, with Deeney and Odion Ighalo proving an effective attacking duo.

There was an even bigger prize at stake for City on this occasion and they did look a little nervy in the first half. Ranieri again showed his tactical bravery by making two substitutions at half-time when the game was still on a knife-edge. Marc Albrighton could feel aggrieved at being taken off as he had played well in the first half, but Ranieri wanted an extra central midfielder on, in the form of Andy King, plus the power and pace of Jeff Schlupp on the left flank. It worked a treat. King played his part in the goal, releasing Christian Fuchs down the left and when the Austrian's cross was cleared by the Watford defence, Riyad Mahrez picked up the ball, danced inside two defenders and drilled home the winner from the edge of the box. The magician, as defender Danny Simpson called Mahrez, had pulled another rabbit out of the hat.

City were five points clear at the top of the table but still there were those who doubted City's title credentials, although they were growing fewer and fewer with every win.

'No one gave us a chance at the start of the season,' said Jamie Vardy after the win at Watford. 'Everyone said we were relegation fodder. It was every newspaper and every pundit, wasn't it? The pressure that we had was up until we knew we were safe. Now we're just enjoying it. Simple as that.

'We've been on a good ride and we're just going to keep enjoying it as it is. We're just taking each game as it comes and no one expected us to be top so we're just enjoying our football and doing what we've always done which is work hard for each other. There is still a long way to go and you will always have doubters no matter how far you go.'

Vardy, teammate Robert Huth and manager Claudio Ranieri were all nominated for the monthly Premier League awards, but missed out as Spurs manager Mauricio Pochettino and Southampton goalkeeper Fraser Foster picked up the awards. Ranieri may have missed out on yet another accolade but those who doubted his credentials when he was appointed as City boss were now acknowledging what a job he was doing.

Earlier in the season, it had been City's attacking mavericks who were stealing all the headlines. City were free-scoring with Vardy and Mahrez in magnificent form, but at the back City were shipping goals. It took ten games for City to keep their first clean sheet, despite Ranieri's offer of pizza; in general, it was a case of City outscoring their opponents. Ranieri had admitted that this was most un-Italian. However, City's defence was now starting to take centre stage. Chances had been at a premium at Watford, but as long as City could keep it tight at the back they knew they always had the potential of snatching a winner, and so it proved.

One of City's most consistent performers was left-back Christian Fuchs. The Austria captain had been signed by Pearson on a free transfer from Bundesliga side Schalke, but then didn't get the chance to undergo a single training session under Pearson's reign. Fuchs had experienced the Champions League at Schalke but had chosen to take up the challenge of what was predicted to be a Premier League relegation battle with City, knowing it would be his swansong as a player in Europe, as he wished to join his family in New York and either play in the MLS or possibly even try his hand at becoming an NFL kicker.

The NFL was popular among several of the City players, particularly Fuchs and Schmeichel. City had forged a bond with the Carolina Panthers as both clubs were defying the odds and flying the flag for the underdogs in their respective leagues. The Panthers had been the surprise package in American Football and City, seemingly noticing the similarities between the two teams' seasons, had sent the Panthers four shirts with the names and numbers of quarterback Cam Newton, cornerback Josh Norman, middle linebacker Luke Kuechly and kicker Graham Gano on the back. The Panthers players had donned the shirts for photos and the Panthers reciprocated by sending shirts for Fuchs and Schmeichel as well as mutual messages of support. Fuchs had loved that. Schmeichel, a New England Patriots fan, was visibly moved as well when patriots quarterback Tom Brady sent him a video message wishing City the best in their title challenge.

Fuchs's wife, Raluca Gold-Fuchs, had gone from being a senior analyst at Goldman Sachs to heading up an event management company. Based permanently in Manhattan with their one-year-old son Anthony and her seven-year-old son Ethan, they were only able to travel to see Fuchs once a month.

'Before I got an offer from Leicester I had an offer to play in America,' Fuchs said. 'I have a family in Manhattan and life is not cheap there. Going to America would not have been a good decision financially for the family because of the nature of the city. I wanted to get everything secure before moving there. That is my responsibility to the family.

'I get to see my family once a month. My wife is doing all the travelling right now. It is tough but essential right now. My intention is to play in the US. I have come for three years. I decided that I would sign one last contract in Europe, when I left Schalke, and then go to the US.'

It may be because he is alone in Leicester but it is fair to say Fuchs is always looking to keep himself busy. While some players avoid social media, Fuchs has embraced it with constant videos and challenges, all under the slogan 'No Fuchs Given', which is more of an attitude than a mere catch-phrase. Fuchs has already taken on City teammate Gökhan Inler in an international skills challenge ahead of a clash between Inler's Switzerland and Fuchs' Austria, and Robert Huth faced Fuchs in a challenge to see who could belt the ball the hardest at the other's backside. 'I am having fun doing it but it is also an attitude,' says Fuchs. 'I like to do it that way. I like to show that attitude, No Fuchs Given.'

Born in Neunkirchen in Lower Austria, Fuchs was encouraged to play football from the moment he started to run. His father, who had been a goalkeeper at amateur level, was the president of SVg Pitten, a local non-league club, and Fuchs, who was originally a striker, joined at a young age before moving on to Wiener Neustadt aged 11. It wasn't an academy education in the conventional sense. Fuchs went to a mainstream school and valued his education, playing at the weekends, competing against adults from the age of 15, but he became a professional aged 17 when he signed for Mattersburg.

'If I had had the chance to go to an academy I might have done it, but I think it helped me much more on a phys-ical level,' says Fuchs. 'It only shows kids that if you can't make it in an academy there is another way. I got a lot of feedback when I was with Mattersburg from parents who would come up to me in the street and say that their son had not been in an academy but wanted to follow my way.

'You need a mix of things: determination, attitude, ability, and positive thinking is important. Just keep going. I spent five years at Mattersburg. We were pretty competitive back then. We had some big names from Austria in the team. We had a pretty good team with good guys. We finished in the top three and played in Europe, which was amazing for a small club like

Mattersburg. There were 6,000 people living in the city, but we always had 17,000 in the stadium, which is humungous for Austria. We had the best average attendance in the whole country in a small town like that. Good memories.'

But Fuchs wanted to spread his wings, like the eagle emblem of Austria, and a move to Bochum in the German Bundesliga beckoned. 'At some point I wanted to make a move abroad,' he said. 'As nice as Austria was it was still limited, in every aspect you can imagine. I was looking for more and before Euro 2008 I signed for Bochum. It was a good move because it wasn't the biggest club but a club where you can show off your skills and talent to bigger clubs. I spent two years at Bochum and then one year at Mainz, which I suppose you could compare to Leicester because we were a small team in a big league that had just got promoted and we finished in the top five.'

Fuchs then moved to Schalke and enjoyed mixed fortunes. He played in the Champions League but also had to overcome a serious knee injury. When his contract was up in Germany he had plenty of offers. As the captain of Austria he was in demand, but he chose Leicester as his final stop before he makes the USA his permanent home.

Fuchs said he was enjoying a fantastic finale to the European leg of his career – and that the extraordinary story of City's rise had been a hot topic even in Manhattan, on his trips over there.

'I feel the interest in Manhattan,' he said. 'There are so many people coming over to me, saying, 'Hey, Leicester.' It is insane. A friend of mine works in the Apple store in Manhattan, the Upper West Side, and he makes sure all the Leicester games are on in the store. Leicester are everyone's second favourite team at least, if not their favourite team. It isn't only our friends – they go crazy for Leicester.

'This should not be happening but that is the beauty of it: that it can happen. I think it is something really good for the league itself. It is something different, something people are getting excited about, not just in England but around the world. Now we want to achieve something unbelievable.'

LEICESTER MERCURY BLOG, 12 MARCH 2016
METHOD IN THE MADNESS

Claudio Ranieri has always been a humorous man, but the difference now is that journalists are laughing with him and not at him.

When he was manager of Chelsea there were times when he was mocked as 'Clownio' in some quarters because of his cartoonish use of English. The derision was more cynical at times as his managerial decisions were openly questioned, but there was more respect for him after the dignified way he handled himself as his time at Chelsea came to an end, with Roman Abramovich openly seeking his successor. He knew he was a dead man walking but faced his situation gracefully.

While he was ridiculed by many, I have not met a journalist who knew him from the early noughties who didn't like him.

Ranieri doesn't care if people think he is ridiculous at times. He was teased for wearing a baseball cap and tracksuit top over his suit in the rain at Bournemouth earlier in the season, but it didn't bother him, not one bit.

Now Ranieri is having the last laugh with Leicester and that comic touch is proving to be an important part of his managerial arsenal.

There hasn't been a press conference this season where there hasn't been a moment of mirth. We have had pizzas and hot dogs bribes, with the Blue Army being described as the tomato sauce on the pizza: 'Without the tomato there is no pizza!'

The latest offering from Ranieri has eclipsed all before it. I defy anyone not to laugh at the sight of Ranieri waving an imaginary bell and saying 'a dilly-ding, dilly-dong'. How many football managers would do that? None. Ranieri is unique.

City have approached this season in a happy-go-lucky fashion, and that has stemmed from Ranieri's approach.

It is a clever tactic and it has had a big effect, not just on the players but on the reporters as well. Nigel Pearson had an uneasy relationship with some sections of the media. He understood the media and knew what they were after but he would often flatly refuse to play the media game.

Ranieri has spent most of his career under an intense media spotlight and he knows what is required. Journalists are looking for a soundbite, a line and a hook to hang their report on. Ranieri provides it, whether it is pizzas or bell-ringing, and the journalists are happy. They have what they want and further questioning is not required. Press conference over, job done. Ranieri has the journalists on his side and has avoided difficult questioning.

When you examine closely how Ranieri conducts himself you can see there is a great deal of intelligence in his approach. He is far from the clown he has been portrayed as in the past.

As Shakespeare said (that's William, not Craig), there is method in his madness.

Next up for City was the visit of struggling Newcastle United. Defeats at the hands of Leicester had seen the end of Garry Monk's and José Mourinho's managerial reigns at Swansea City and Chelsea respectively. This would be a different situation as the Magpies had already changed their manager, turning to former Liverpool and Real Madrid manager Rafa Benítez in the hope that he could save them from relegation. The Spaniard was taking charge of his new club for the first time at the King Power Stadium, so there was an element of facing the unknown for Ranieri's men. Newcastle, though, had lost their last three league games, and had lost 17 of their last 21 Premier League away matches. They had scored just eight goals in their last 20 away games, failing to score in 13 of those. But Benitez's appointment had placed a wild card in the pack.

Newcastle were also being held up as a classic example of how not to close out a title challenge. In 1996, Kevin Keegan's side had blown a 12-point lead at the top. Tottenham had cut City's lead to just two points with a 2-0 win at Aston Villa the day before, to apply a bit of pressure to Ranieri's men.

Before the game, former City favourite Gary Lineker, who admitted he got it terribly wrong when he questioned the appointment of Ranieri at the start of the season, said the current players would become immortals if they could do what Newcastle could not 19 years before and join the select group of Premier League champions. They were about to take another impressive step towards it.

It was a forgettable game, settled by an unforgettable goal. Shinji Okazaki's overhead kick in the first half was sensational, a goal fit to win any game. For Okazaki's previous five goals, the tenacious little Japan international had bustled, bundled and barged the ball over the line; but against

Newcastle his bicycle kick from Jamie Vardy's cushioned header was sublime.

With City now at their obstinate best defensively the Geordies could find no way back. The gap was back to five points after another 1-0 win. It was to become a common theme. City headed down to Crystal Palace next and it was the same story as at Watford. City weren't at their bristling best but defensively they were solid and Mahrez repeated his match-winning feats, with Vardy the provider again. City fans were starting to really believe their team were on their way to the title, refusing to leave Selhurst Park for at least 20 minutes after the final whistle. 'We're gonna win the league, and now you're going to believe us,' they sang with gusto. The chorus seemed even louder as Selhurst Park was now empty and the acoustics echoed around the open ground. Eventually, Palace officials, very politely, issued an announcement across the PA thanking Leicester fans for their support and urging them to vacate the stadium. 'We shall not, we shall not be moved,' was the light-hearted reply. Eventually, they did leave to embark on the long journey back up the M1, but they could have floated home, so great was the euphoria.

As consistent as the 1-0 scoreline was City's starting line-up. City had made the fewest changes to their team in the Premier League by some distance. Ranieri was not living up to his Tinkerman reputation. 'If I see somebody a little tired during a game or a training session, maybe I can change,' he said. 'I moved a lot of players only in the last season at Chelsea when new players arrived after the start of the Premier League. [Roman] Abramovich came in at the beginning of July and at that point we started to buy new players, so it was normal that I changed players. Because of that I was the Tinkerman, but that is okay because I changed a lot. New players arrived so I had to put in new players and we finished second.

'Some players start to play straight away in the Premier League but other players need more time. Then you have to change things and move things. I changed systems in 1997 and 1998, a long time ago. Now all around the world people change systems and change men. Now everybody is a Tinkerman but the flag is mine. I was the first!'

Now Ranieri's reputation was at its highest. His achievement in turning a team like City into title contenders had led to speculation that bigger clubs and even the Italian FA wanted him, but he declared he wanted to end his illustrious career in charge of the Foxes.

'I want to stay here,' Ranieri insisted. 'I am so happy here, there is so much to do – we are just starting to build. If the owner is happy with me, I'm happy with him. I'd like this to be my last job – yes, if it's possible I'd like to be here a long time. No team can change my mind. Definitely no! Of course I am very proud if they are thinking of me in Italy or anywhere else, but this is my club.'

LEICESTER MERCURY BLOG, 23 MARCH 2016
RAGS TO RICHES

This week has really driven home the gravitas of what Leicester City are achieving this season.

Last weekend they went to Crystal Palace and ground out another crucial 1-0 win to heap the pressure back on Tottenham Hotspur, who to their credit responded to make this an intriguing, enthralling title race.

That's four 1-0 wins in the last five games. That is a trait that previous champions have displayed.

Normally when watching City you always feel a little

apprehensive when they are defending a one-goal advantage away from home. In the past they have invited pressure and the inevitable has happened, but not this season.

There was a new confidence that City would not wilt, that they would stand strong, and it never felt like they would concede.

At the end, while the Blue Army were singing 'We're going to win the league' at one end of the ground, the gracious Palace fans were applauding the City players off the pitch.

City are now everyone's second favourite team because people have fallen in love with the romance of their rags-to-riches story.

It feels like everyone is willing City on to finish the job and complete the most remarkable, astonishing of title triumphs. City are feeling the love.

On Wednesday there was the surreal moment when I watched, along with a lot of City fans I am sure, the press conference live from New York City when Leicester were announced as participants in the American leg of the International Champions Cup along with Barcelona, AC Milan, Inter Milan, Paris Saint-Germain, Bayern Munich, Chelsea, Liverpool and Celtic.

It was announced City will play PSG in Los Angeles and Barcelona in Stockholm during this prestigious pre-season tournament. What a difference that will be, because all the pre-seasons I have experienced following City over the past seven years, except the Sven-Göran Eriksson days when City took on Real Madrid after tours of Sweden and Austria, have involved trips to Ilkeston Town, Lincoln City, York City and Burton Albion.

A representative from each club, mostly former club legends, took turns to address the press conference. There was

Emilio Butragueño for Real Madrid, Edgar Davids for Inter, Youri Djorkaeff for PSG and then, last but by no means least, our own Alan Birchenall, who stole the show by turning to the illustrious dignitaries from some of the greatest clubs in the world and said: 'It is apt I am last up because a year ago we were last in the Premier League, but we are catching you lot up!'

This was Leicester City. Yes, Leicester City being represented alongside such giants of the game, but that is what the club has aspired to do under the ownership of the Srivaddhanaprabha family.

When Vichai said in Bangkok nearly two years ago that he had a three-year plan to see City competing in the top six of the Premier League season, estimating it would cost an investment of £180 million to achieve it, I bet many people outside Leicester laughed, but City fans must have been impressed by his ambition. He has been true to his word. In fact, City are ahead of schedule.

After watching the live streaming of the press conference I headed off to St George's Park, the impressive rural training base for all the England national teams, to see City duo Danny Drinkwater and Jamie Vardy face the media ahead of the international friendlies against Germany and Holland. For Vardy it wasn't a new experience but for Drinkwater it was. He had been dreaming about being on England duty since he was a boy and now his time has come.

It has been thoroughly deserved, in my opinion. Drinkwater's rise has mirrored City's in many ways. Last season City were bottom of the table and Drinkwater was out of the team, behind Esteban Cambiasso, Matty James and Andy King in the pecking order.

When Cambiasso decided he wasn't re-signing the big question was how City would fill the void. Cambiasso was a huge favourite with the fans and a big influence within the squad. Ranieri said he wanted a champion to replace him. Gökhan Inler arrived shortly afterwards, but it has been Drinkwater, and not N'Golo Kanté, who has filled that role. Kanté is a very different player, but it is Drinkwater who has assumed the Cambiasso role.

During the press conference, Vardy declared that Drinkwater was 'the Puppet Master' because he pulls all the strings, just like Cambiasso did.

They sat side by side at a table on a small stage and faced the national press pack and they were like Morecambe and Wise. Drinkwater was Wise and Vardy was Morecambe. While Drinkwater dealt with all the questions with a straight bat, Vardy added the comic touch, declaring the film-maker plotting a film about his life as 'mad'.

Drinky was dubbed as a complicated character by Nigel Pearson and while he comes across much more relaxed and confident this season, in the past he has seemed very intense. Right now he seems a lot more comfortable and happy with life.

It was great to see two City players being the centre of attention and wearing the Three Lions. Just a few years ago that never seemed possible. That is how far City has come.

The fact they have devoted such time on a national radio station to the club just shows everyone is talking about Leicester City.

Most people connected to Leicester City probably didn't want the international break that followed, fearing momentum could be lost. Danny Drinkwater was the exception. His stunning performances for City had led to a call-up to the England squad for the friendlies against Germany in Berlin and against Holland at Wembley.

I remember the first time I met Danny Drinkwater. It was a Saturday morning, 21 January 2012. City didn't have a game as they were away to Southampton on the Monday night. Drinkwater had officially joined Leicester City from Manchester United the day before, for a fee believed to be around £1 million.

Manchester born and bred, Drinkwater had been at United from the age of nine. He had worked his way through the ranks but never made a first-team appearance. The closest he came was when he was named as a substitute for a game against Hull City at the end of the 2008/09 season, but he didn't get on. He didn't fulfil that dream.

He had been farmed out on loan to Huddersfield Town, Watford, Cardiff City and Barnsley. It was in a game for the Tykes that I first noticed him in action. It was just a week before he joined City and he was outstanding as Barnsley won 2-1 at the King Power Stadium. Andy Gray may have scored both goals but it was Drinkwater who really caught the eye. It was probably the performance that convinced Nigel Pearson this 20-year-old would be a good fit for City.

I met him in an upstairs players' lounge at Belvoir Drive. He had been schooled at United's highly acclaimed academy but he seemed nervous as I interviewed him, giving brief answers and appearing suspicious of certain questions; but he came across as a good lad, one who probably preferred to do his talking on the pitch. That was exactly what he did during the Championship title-winning season, choosing not to do any media as he didn't want to jinx his great season.

It didn't go brilliantly for him at the start. I remember a midweek game at Watford three weeks after he joined. City lost 3-2. The press bench at Vicarage Road was just a few metres from the away dugout, so I could clearly hear every instruction Pearson and Craig Shakespeare barked out from the technical area. Drinkwater seemed to be the focus of it as they grew increasingly frustrated. Pearson wanted Drinkwater to screen the back four, but he wasn't getting it right. He was substituted just after half-time for Neil Danns.

Five years later and Drinkwater is no longer that nervous boy I first met. He is a man, one of the leaders in the City dressing room, an established Premier League player and England international. He has worked incredibly hard on his game, to improve in every area. When I watch him now he looks like the complete midfielder. His range of passing is exceptional, he works incredibly hard and makes telling, driving runs forward. He even screens the back four properly. The one thing he needed to add to his game was a few more goals, and he has done that with goals against Stoke City and West Bromwich Albion. (Okay, they were both deflections, but you can't win the lottery if you don't buy a ticket.) He is also much more confident in front of the press, which is so important at international level where the spotlight is so intense. He is very honest in his answers to questions, copes well with the trickier ones, and even cracks a joke in his dry style.

Pearson once said he was a complicated character, but he seems to be thriving now under Claudio Ranieri, having spent a frustrating first season in the Premier League behind Esteban Cambiasso and Matty James. Drinkwater has emerged as the midfield 'champion' City had been looking for in the summer.

But it was to be Vardy who stole the show as England recorded a famous win over the world champions on their own turf, scoring his first international goal with a deft near-post flick, and he would score his first goal at Wembley a few days later in a defeat to the Dutch. Not to be outdone, Drinkwater earned the man-of-the-match award on his debut at the home of English football. It completed a memorable journey for the Manchester lad.

Kanté also made his mark on the international stage, scoring for France on his debut against Russia, while Shinji Okazaki scored a great goal for Japan.

MARCH SUMMARY

Competition	Date	Fixture
Premier League	Tue 1 Mar	Leicester 2-2 West Brom
Premier League	Sat 5 Mar	Watford 0-1 Leicester
Premier League	Mon 14 Mar	Leicester 1-0 Newcastle
Premier League	Sat 19 Mar	Crystal Palace 0-1 Leicester

*The Foxes now had to contend with the added pressure
of being favourites, but after an unexpected draw against
West Brom, they began a relentless run of form:*

*Evens – 14 March (after winning at home to Newcastle;
Manchester City had drawn away at Norwich on the 12th,
while Spurs had won away at Aston Villa on the 13th)*

8-15 – 19 March (after winning at Crystal Palace)

APRIL 2016

		P	W	D	L	GF	GA	GD	Pts
1	Leicester City	31	19	9	3	54	31	23	66
2	Tottenham Hotspur	31	17	10	4	56	24	32	61
3	Arsenal	30	16	7	7	48	30	18	55
4	Manchester City	30	15	6	9	52	32	20	51

Standings on 1 April

City had secured their Premier League status against Sunderland at the Stadium of Light a year before. The game ended 0-0 and was instantly forgettable, but the celebrations will be remembered by City fans forever. This time City were on a completely different mission as they headed to Wearside. They were fighting not for survival, but for the title, and they gave a performance befitting their status as potential champions. The week before, Wes Morgan had scored the winner against Southampton at the King Power Stadium as City recorded their fourth 1-0 win on the trot. Now, on Wearside, City controlled the game, taking the lead when Drinkwater set Vardy free behind the Black Cats' defence and the number 9 produced an emphatic finish, becoming the first City striker to reach the milestone of 20 goals in a season in the top flight since Gary Lineker in 1984/85. Jack Rodwell let City off with a woeful effort when the goal was gaping, before Vardy sealed the win, racing clear of the Sunderland defence once more and rounding keeper Vito Mannone before rolling the ball into the empty net.

City were now just three wins away from winning the title and as the travelling City fans celebrated in the upper tier of the stands, again refusing to leave the ground, Ranieri looked overcome with emotion. Was that a tear in his eye?

'You make this job for the emotion you feel inside, but it is difficult for me to tell what kind of emotion,' said Ranieri afterwards. 'It is fantastic when you see, before the match, an old lady with a Leicester shirt outside the stadium. I say, "Unbelievable. They come from Leicester to support us." This is my emotion. It is fantastic. That is football.'

⚽

LEICESTER MERCURY BLOG, 11 APRIL 2016
RAW EMOTION

It was a fantastic weekend for the sporting underdog.

Rule the World, a 33-1 shot, won the Grand National on Saturday before Danny Willett, a relative unknown and a 66-1 shot ahead of the tournament, won the Masters at Augusta on Sunday night. In fact, at the end of January you could have got odds of 150-1 on the Sheffield golfer pulling on the green jacket.

And, of course, the biggest underdogs of them all, Leicester City, the 5000-1 rank outsiders for the Premier League title, took another significant step towards what would be the most unbelievable and miraculous sporting triumph of all.

It is enough to bring a tear to a grown man's eye, and that was exactly what happened at the final whistle at the Stadium of Light when City boss Claudio Ranieri looked up proudly to the massed ranks of the Blue Army in the upper tier of the stand following City's 2-0 victory.

Despite 30 years of experience as a coach, the Italian seemed to struggle to contain his emotions. It is a completely understandable reaction to what is rapidly becoming the most romantic of sporting fairy-tales.

City are now tantalisingly close to becoming English champions in an era of football when no side other than the mega-rich elite are supposed to become champions, and having been so close on so many occasions in Italy, Spain and England, the perennial bridesmaid is now close to finally being the bride.

His raw display of emotion will endear him even further to the Blue Army who probably already want Ranieri sainted for what he has achieved for City so far. There have already been calls from a Leicestershire MP for Ranieri to be knighted.

After the game Ranieri had composed himself and said City must keep their focus and concentration because the job isn't done. It is time to wipe away the Italian tear and put on an English stiff upper lip because there is still plenty of work to do. Tottenham Hotspur demonstrated a few hours later that they have not given up the chase.

Judging by the way the players spoke after the game at the Stadium of Light there was no evidence that this remarkable title race was taking its toll on them. In fact, with every game that passes it is remarkable to see how players like Jamie Vardy, Danny Drinkwater and Marc Albrighton, who all stopped to speak after the game, are taking this all in their stride.

The manager may be displaying his emotions, but the players seem so relaxed and confident that those who are still waiting for City to fold like a pack of cards may be waiting a long time. The players have been the same all season long. There was no difference in their body language, the tone or sentiment of what they said after this win over Sunderland, than there was after the opening day of the season win over the Black Cats at the King Power Stadium.

To so many of us inside the stadium, including it seemed Ranieri, it felt like a significant moment, but to the players it was just another game, another win, another clean sheet, another three points and another step closer to their goal.

They seem to just be ticking off the victories and now they are just three away with five games remaining.

If they do it, there will be a few more tears and a few more people across Leicestershire who will struggle to contain their emotions.

⚽

THE TWIST IN THE TALE

You get a feeling it could be a strange day when you awake to ice and snow on the ground in mid-April.

Fans arriving at the King Power Stadium ahead of the visit of West Ham may have found the presence of a gospel choir outside the ground, singing terrace songs honouring Claudio Ranieri and his men, a little surreal too.

However, the sight and sound of a referee leaving the field to whistles, boos and catcalls from both sets of fans was extraordinary. Usually, it is just one set of fans that are incensed, not the whole ground. Referee Jonathan Moss had just awarded City a last-minute penalty which Leonardo Ulloa had converted to snatch what could yet prove to be a crucial point for Claudio Ranieri's men but that did nothing to appease nearly 30,000 City fans who vented their anger in the official's direction as he left the field.

City had started the day seven points clear at the top of the table and another victory – which would have been City's sixth on the trot – would have heaped more pressure on rivals Tottenham Hotspur, who were again playing 24 hours after City.

Everything seemed to be going to plan and there was a familiar feel to the game as City soaked up early pressure from a Hammers side still chasing European football qualification, and scored a classic counter-attacking goal.

Kasper Schmeichel easily gathered Dimitri Payet's free-kick and immediately released Riyad Mahrez, who picked out N'Golo Kanté's typical bursting run down the middle. The Frenchman teed up Jamie Vardy, who flashed an unstoppable left-footed strike past goalkeeper Adrián to score goal number 22 for the season. From the moment Schmeichel gathered the ball to the moment Vardy's shot flashed past Adrián took just 13 seconds.

The second half was dominated by controversial moments and while Vardy would still be centre stage, he would share the limelight with Moss.

As he had done at Sunderland, Danny Drinkwater picked up a loose ball in midfield and immediately released Vardy with a ball over the top. Vardy had Angelo Ogbonna in hot pursuit and the pair were side by side inside the area when they both came crashing to the ground. Moss blew his whistle. The City fans called for a penalty while Vardy sat up and looked in Moss's direction in anticipation. It seemed like an eternity before he indicated no penalty. Even worse for Vardy, he decided that not only had the City striker instigated the contact, but that the offence was worthy of a second yellow card. Vardy was off, but not before he had told Moss, in no uncertain terms, what he thought of the decision – an act that would have further consequences for City.

While many would later say Vardy had been unlucky with his first booking in the first half, for an innocuous-looking foul on Cheikhou Kouyaté, most of the journalists and pundits, as well as West Ham United manager Slaven Bilić, would agree with Moss that Vardy had been looking for the penalty, although Vardy would receive support later in the week from England manager Roy Hodgson and Ranieri, who both felt it was merely a coming together and that Vardy had been unlucky.

The City crowd now turned on Moss as their hero, Vardy, left the field and the referee further entrenched himself in their bad books by penalising Wes Morgan for a pull on Winston Reid at a Hammers corner and awarded the visitors a controversial penalty.

Players from both sides had been grappling at set-pieces. It had resembled a wrestling match at times, but both sides were culpable. But Moss decided enough was enough with just six minutes remaining and it was City who bore the brunt of his decision. Substitute Andy Carroll stepped up and fired home the equaliser from the spot. It was the first goal City had conceded in nearly ten hours of action.

Two minutes later and the Hammers were ahead. With all the controversy in the wake of the game it would be almost forgotten that Aaron Cresswell had put the visitors in front with a superb finish. Kasper Schmeichel's stunning finger-tip save in the first two minutes when he pushed Kouyaté's header on to the near post, and then watched as it bounced along his goal-line, striking the inside of the opposite post before rolling back into his arms, would also be lost in all the vitriol of the post-match analysis.

Still, the game wasn't over. With just ten men and with time running out, City appeared to be heading for a defeat that would present Spurs with an opportunity to strike a psychological blow in their next game, at Stoke's Britannia Stadium, but in the last minute of the game Moss made one more decision. When Carroll clumsily bundled into Jeff Schlupp just inside the right-hand side of the Hammers box, Moss blew his whistle again and pointed to the penalty spot.

Robert Huth had been bundled to the ground as the grappling theme had continued just moments before but Moss had waved away City's increasingly vehement appeals only now to give arguably the softest penalty of the lot. Ulloa had scored some famous, earth-shaking, late goals but none seem as important as when he slotted home the spot-kick to give City a point.

Seconds later, Moss blew his whistle for the last time, but it would not be his last act as his post-match report would have ramifications for City and Vardy. Initially, the City fans celebrated, as it felt like a reprieve with defeat having looked so likely, but that soon was replaced with blind fury as Moss was escorted from the pitch. Huth tried to have a word but was pulled away, while Marcin Wasilewski just stood and stared as Moss, surrounded by security guards, ran the gauntlet towards the sanctuary of the tunnel.

All City fans had known there would be a twist in the tale at some point in what was emerging as an enthralling title chase, but never did they think there would be so many of them in one half of one game.

LEICESTER MERCURY BLOG, 18 APRIL 2016
A STRIKING DILEMMA

The fall-out from the actions of referee Jonathan Moss during Leicester City's controversial draw with West Ham United on Sunday could have a dramatic effect on the Premier League title race.

Moss's decision to show Jamie Vardy a second yellow card for diving did not just have a bearing on the outcome of the game, it could have a big impact on the destiny of the title itself.

Had he simply waved play on after Vardy went down following a clash with Angelo Ogbonna, it was likely that City would have gone on to claim another home win and edged closer to becoming champions of England for the first time in the club's history.

However, his decision not only reduced City to ten men and gave the Hammers the initiative to take control of the game, and ultimately deny City the win, it left City without their main striker and top scorer.

It now means City not only have to face Swansea City next Sunday without Vardy for the first time in the league this season, they could also be forced to change the way they play.

It could get even worse for City as well, after Vardy accepted a charge of improper conduct for his behaviour after the red card, although he will plead his case after requesting a personal hearing. If the one-game ban is increased Vardy could miss the trip to Old Trafford to face Manchester United as well.

Claudio Ranieri has hinted that Leonardo Ulloa will replace Vardy against Swansea. The Argentinian showed his unwavering temperament by stepping up to fire home City's last-minute equaliser from the penalty spot with regular penalty taker Vardy off the pitch.

However, Ulloa is a very different player to Vardy. While Vardy has proved such a valuable outlet for City with his ability to run the channels, race in behind defenders and stretch the pitch, Ulloa is a touch player, more comfortable with his back to goal and bringing others into play before getting into the box.

City will not be able to suck teams in before breaking on them as effectively as they have all season.

There are alternatives. Ulloa could play in the more withdrawn striking role and allow Shinji Okazaki to play off the shoulder of the last defender, while Jeff Schlupp's pace, power and directness makes him a more natural, like-for-like replacement for Vardy.

It will be interesting to see in which direction Claudio Ranieri goes because it is a crucial decision. Regardless, Vardy will be a huge loss for City. He has been integral to City's phenomenal season. There have been so many valuable contributions from everyone in the squad, but Vardy's

22 goals and six assists tell their own story. He is City's key man, the talisman.

Spurs' title challenge would be severely dented if they lost Harry Kane at such a crucial time. Vardy is City's Kane.

Spurs took advantage with a comprehensive win over Stoke City at the Britannia Stadium on the Monday night and the gap was reduced to five points with four games remaining. City still had a healthy advantage but Spurs were putting them under pressure. After City's draw with the Hammers, Spurs striker Harry Kane put a cryptic picture of some lions on the prowl on Instagram, which was interpreted as a message being sent to City that Spurs smelt blood and were on the hunt.

The Foxes of Leicester have a proud hunting tradition. The Post Horn Gallop has been played as the players have emerged from the tunnel before every game since 1941, symbolic of the Foxes being chased out of the tunnel on to the pitch. Now it was Spurs doing the chasing.

Not that Ranieri was losing his cool. His pre-match press conference ahead of the Swansea game was a masterclass as he deflected attention from the controversy of the West Ham game by finally declaring City were now in a hunt of their own, for the title.

'We are in the Champions League, man! Dilly-ding, dilly-dong! Come on man,' he cried, interrupting the journalist's more sombre questioning. 'It's fantastic, terrific, well done to everybody. It's a great achievement – unbelievable. Now, we go straight away to try to win the title. Only this remains. Mauricio, keep calm!'

If Spurs thought the pressure was now directly on City,

Ranieri had other ideas. 'I don't need to win all the matches; they need to win all their matches – we don't. We have everything in our hands. I prefer my position to Spurs'. We have to push a lot and believe a lot and push with our heart and soul. Carry on and keep going, smiling, and fight, try, believe; if it happens – fireworks.'

As for losing key man Vardy for at least one game, Ranieri said he had lost his 'Caesar', but that he had 23 other Caesars to step in. Four of his Caesars had been named in the PFA team of the year, which was leaked online. Morgan, Kanté, Mahrez and Vardy were all included, while Kanté, Mahrez and Vardy were nominated for the PFA player of the year award.

All the talk before the visit of Swansea was about how Leicester were to cope without talisman striker Vardy. He hadn't missed a league game all season, so who would score the goals in his absence? Leicester provided an unequivocal answer, thrashing the Swans 4-0 to put the pressure back on Spurs, who were again in action the next night, against West Bromwich Albion.

With Vardy watching from the stands Leicester needed their other star man Mahrez to return to form and he duly obliged, capitalising on a horrendous mistake from Ashley Williams to score the first goal.

Leonardo Ulloa, who had come in for Vardy, then took centre stage, scoring with a thumping header in the first half and sliding in to score his second from Jeff Schlupp's pass after the break. Then all three of Leicester's substitutes combined for the fourth as Demarai Gray and Andy King combined before Marc Albrighton fired home. 'Four-nil to the one-man team,' the City fans sang.

Shortly after the game the City squad and Ranieri were flown by helicopter down to London for the PFA player of the year awards ceremony at the Grosvenor Hotel – although Gray nearly didn't make it as he had to be saved from walking accidentally into a rotary blade. This wasn't a time for losing one's head.

It was a famous night for City. As well as the four players in the Premier League team of the year, Vardy was presented with a special award for setting a new Premier League record of scoring in 11 consecutive games, and Mahrez was named the players' player of the year, receiving the award from Ranieri.

Life had certainly changed over the past 12 months for Mahrez. He had become father to a daughter before Christmas and his stunning performances had meant he was no longer anonymous. He was the rising star of English football. When he had first arrived at City he could be seen heading out after a game for a late-night kebab in a local restaurant, but that was impossible now, as was a simple trip to the nearby shopping centre.

'I did that a couple of times, but not for a long time,' he said of his kebab days. 'Now I go home and my wife cooks for me.

'After you have run you need the energy so I need to eat. I used to eat takeaways when I was young, like kebabs. Sometimes you go and eat, but it was a long time ago now. I am still skinny.

'It has changed a lot this year. Last year I could go to the shopping centre and some people take some pictures and ask for autographs but I can't now. It is too much. I know they love us. I love them as well but I can't go out with my wife and my baby to the shopping centre. Everyone comes around us, but it is still good and we love the fact they are happy.'

The PFA award was another remarkable stop on his incredible journey from the streets of Parisian suburb

Sarcelles to the echelons of the Premier League. Mahrez had only signed his first professional contract with Le Havre six years before but the 25-year-old said he always believed he would make it as a professional.

'My dream was to be a professional and I always believed I would, always,' he said. 'I never give up. Even when I was playing for Sarcelles and Quimper I felt I would be a professional. I believed I could. I just wanted to play football.

'This is my best season, of course; I just started football four or five years ago – this is the best. Maybe I didn't think I would score as many goals. I knew I could score goals but not a lot like this season. I thought 10 or 12, now it is 16, it is a lot. But the job is not finished and I can still score a couple more. I will focus to help my team to win so I can score or give an assist. A season like this you are always surprised because no one was expecting this.

'I would prefer to win the title even if I am not a big player. The first thing is the team and then after, yes, to be part of things and score a lot of goals, and assists, of course I am proud of it, but I don't think too much about me, just the team. It is good to hear people say nice things about me, especially from good players, but I don't want to speak too much about me. The team is the most important thing and then afterwards if I receive some awards it would be good, but it is not my objective.'

The contrast from the mood around City following the controversial draw with the Hammers to the euphoria of the Swansea win and Mahrez's award was astonishing, and there was to be another twist when Spurs took on West Brom at White Hart Lane.

Spurs simply couldn't afford a slip-up. They were in the last-chance saloon with City now eight points ahead. They were expected to beat Tony Pulis's side and when Craig Dawson scored an unfortunate own goal they were on track. City fans were preparing to go to Manchester United the following Sunday knowing the title race would still be very much alive.

However, the incredible happened and Dawson atoned for his own goal by heading home an equaliser. The roar from Leicester could probably have been heard in north London.

There were many City fans back home who could not watch. Either they thought that by watching they would somehow affect the outcome, or they simply didn't want to know. Leave it to the gods. Whatever will be, will be. However, when Dawson's goal went in there were spontaneous outbursts across the city and county. People in pubs, restaurants, supermarkets, gyms, even just walking down the street, suddenly cried out in delight.

Even the news the next day that the FA had imposed a second one-game ban on Vardy, fined him £10,000 and fined the club £20,000 for the players' reaction to the Hammers' penalty could not stifle their excitement. City were now on the cusp of the greatest achievement in the club's history.

How the fortunes of the title rivals had changed. A week before it was City who had dropped two points on home soil and Spurs who had applied the pressure with a 4-0 win; now the roles were reversed. Moreover, just as City had lost key man Vardy to suspension, Spurs starlet Dele Alli was now banned for the rest of the season for an off-the-ball incident in the West Brom game, when he appeared to stab a punch into the midriff of Claudio Yacob.

Kevin Keegan, Kenny Dalglish, Peter Shilton, Gary Lineker, Alan Shearer, Eric Cantona, Dennis Bergkamp, Thierry Henry, Steven Gerrard, Cristiano Ronaldo, Ryan Giggs, Wayne Rooney, Gareth Bale, Luis Suárez – Riyad Mahrez.

Leicester City's first-ever winner of the PFA players' player of the year award joined some illustrious company when he stepped onto the stage at the Grosvenor Hotel in London last night and received his prize from City boss Claudio Ranieri.

It was another remarkable moment in what has been an astonishing, fairy-tale season for Mahrez and all his City teammates. It is also another incredible chapter in the amazing story of the rise of the street kid from Sarcelles.

Mahrez has come a long way from his first appearance in a City kit, when he scored for the under-21s in an away victory at West Bromwich Albion. Hardly anyone saw Mahrez on that day and not much was known about the 22-year-old when he joined City from French second-tier side Le Havre for £400,000 in January 2014.

City fans had to take then-manager Nigel Pearson's word for it when he said: 'Riyad is a pleasing addition to a squad that already has a lot of quality and I'm delighted we've been able to secure his signature.

'He is a talented player, technically very good, and he gives us another option in attacking positions.'

At the time City fans were already salivating over the performances of City's other French signing, Anthony Knockaert. If Mahrez could turn out to be as good as Knockaert then City fans would have another terrace hero, but he has totally eclipsed his former teammate.

The early indications were promising as Mahrez made a succession of late substitute appearances, scoring his first goal in a 2-2 draw at Nottingham Forest, a crucial late equaliser. Crucial late goals would prove to be his calling card.

He spoke publicly for the first time on the side of the City Ground pitch, with Knockaert acting as his interpreter.

'I am very happy because it is my first goal for the club, it's an important goal and it is a great feeling,' he said, or rather Knockaert said for him.

He had been advised by friends not to play in England, that the physicality of the English game would not suit his style of play as much as in other countries. He had had a trial at St Mirren in Scotland but hated it so much he borrowed a bicycle and fled, leaving his boots behind. But Pearson said Mahrez was a confident lad who could adapt.

'There is no doubt when you come from a different style of league there will be a period of adaptation,' Pearson said. 'You don't get the time on the ball you may get in other leagues, but he is a quick learner and a quality player.'

However, there was no real indication of the player he would become, although inside the City camp Pearson and his coaches felt Mahrez had even more potential than Knockaert, that long-term he would become an even better player. They were to be proven right.

It was six games into his City career that Mahrez made his first start, in the 3-0 home win over Charlton Athletic, and he would go on to score twice more as he forged an effective twin-wing attack with Knockaert as City clinched promotion to the Premier League and the Championship title.

His performances earned him a call-up by Algeria, the country of his late father's origin, and he would cement himself in the Algeria squad, although his first season in the Premier League mirrored City's for a long spell of the campaign – a struggle.

Mahrez scored four times, including both goals in a 2-0 win over Southampton as City won seven of their last nine games to clinch survival. He also provided three assists and signed a new four-year contract in August 2015.

This season has seen Mahrez fulfil that potential that Pearson spoke about when he arrived as an unknown two-and-a-half seasons ago – and then some. No matter how much self-confidence Mahrez may have possessed from the outset, he could have only dared to dream that he would score 17 goals and provide 11 assists in a City side that is closing in on a first-ever English title.

He could scarcely have contemplated that he would also be named Algerian player of the year and PFA player of the year as well. It has been an astonishing transformation, equal to Jamie Vardy's and to City's.

At 25, Mahrez has come of age and the question is no longer who is he? The question now is how good could he be?

LEICESTER MERCURY BLOG, 27 APRIL 2016
RANIERI'S GREATEST ACHIEVEMENT

He has been dubbed the perennial bridesmaid for not being able to close out previous title challenges, but Claudio Ranieri could finally get to be the bride with Leicester City.

Nine times during his illustrious managerial career he has achieved a top-four finish and four times he has finished as runner-up in a domestic title race.

He came close with Chelsea to winning the Premier League in 2004, but was beaten by Arsenal's 'Invincibles'.

With Juventus in 2009, two seasons after 'the Old Lady' had been promoted from Serie B, he led them to second place behind José Mourinho's Inter Milan, although he was sacked two games before the end of the season after falling out with several senior players and members of the club hierarchy.

He was pipped again by Mourinho and Inter a year later as manager of Roma, despite being top of the table with four games remaining. Inter won their last five games to seal the title by two points and also beat Roma in the Italian Cup final, to compound the misery.

Ranieri headed to France where he led Monaco to the Ligue 2 title in his first season, one of three second-tier titles in his career (the others came at Cagliari and Fiorentina), and pushed the dominant force of Paris Saint-Germain for the title in 2014.

However, just as he had experienced at Chelsea, the writing had been on the wall for most of the final few months of that campaign as he struggled to satisfy the growing expectation at Monaco.

Unrealistic expectation has been a feature of all those previous experiences. Chelsea and Monaco were emerging sides but had spent fortunes, while Juventus fans always expect their side to win Serie A, regardless of what shape the club has been in.

Only at Roma was the burden of expectation weighing not quite so heavily on Ranieri's shoulders, but then again Roma, three times Italian champions, are hardly footballing lightweights.

Ranieri has had to put up with ridicule, leading to the bridesmaid tag, from journalists and even Mourinho, who famously teased him for the lack of titles on his CV when the two played out a very public rivalry in Italy, but Ranieri defends his record vehemently.

'Every time, like Leicester now, I know there are people who say if I don't win the title, "Ah, Claudio, he always finishes second". Yes, but if you look at my career I was always behind,' Ranieri says in mitigation.

'At Chelsea, we started to build a team during the previous year. I continued to buy people during the first matches of the Premier League and Champions League, to build everybody, and I arrive second.

'I was second in Rome. What can I do more? I arrived after two matches when we had no points. I made 80 points.

'At Inter Milan I made 82, what can I do? When I arrived at Juventus the team had just come back up from Serie B. We arrived third in the first year and then second. What can I do? I had just four or five champions and the rest were young players.

'At Monaco we won the Serie B second division and we arrived Paris Saint-Germain with 80 points again. No one who finished second made 80 points.

'Now I try to win this. No one expected Leicester City to be in this position. Of course I will not be happy if we arrive second, but what can I do?

'We are doing a fantastic job and we have to keep going in the same way.'

Ranieri has never been so close to a domestic title. City need just three points from their remaining three games to ensure, regardless of what Tottenham Hotspur do, that they win the Premier League and become champions of England for the first time in the club's 132-year history.

Then, the teasing and the patronising will be over, the ribbing will stop. The bridesmaid tag will be dropped for ever.

Ranieri will be able to finally savour the greatest moment of his career. It would be an achievement that would eclipse all others.

Claudio Ranieri will finally be a champion.

City's lead was now seven points with just three games to go. Three more points would guarantee the miracle would be complete.

Next up was Manchester United away. A trip to the Theatre of Dreams.

A City win at Old Trafford and all their dreams would come true.

APRIL SUMMARY

Competition	Date	Fixture
Premier League	Sun 3 Apr	Leicester 1-0 Southampton
Premier League	Sun 10 Apr	Sunderland 0-2 Leicester
Premier League	Sun 17 Apr	Leicester 2-2 West Ham
Premier League	Sun 24 Apr	Leicester 4-0 Swansea

A resounding 4-0 win against Swansea left
Leicester City on the brink of the title:

1-3 – 3 April (after winning at home to Southampton)

1-6 – 10 April (after winning at home to Sunderland;
elsewhere, Spurs won at home to Manchester United)

1-4 – 17 April (after drawing at home with West Ham)

4-9 – 18 April (after Spurs won away at Stoke)

1-6 – 24 April – (after winning at home to Swansea)

1-20 – 25 April (after Spurs drew at home to West Brom)

MAY 2016

		P	W	D	L	GF	GA	GD	Pts
1	Leicester City	35	22	10	3	63	33	30	76
2	Tottenham Hotspur	35	19	12	4	65	26	39	69
3	Arsenal	36	19	10	7	59	34	25	67
4	Manchester City	35	19	7	9	66	34	32	64

Standings on 1 May

THE FAIRY-TALE ENDING DRAWS NEAR

Blue battered sausages and fish? They may not sound the most appetising things but in the spirit of Backing the Blues day, everything in Leicester was taking on a blue hue.

The *Leicester Mercury* and BBC Radio Leicester had launched a campaign encouraging the whole of the city to show their support for Claudio Ranieri and his men as they stood on the cusp of greatness. They didn't need much encouraging.

The fish shop fare wasn't the only tribute to City. Cappuccinos were made featuring the image of Vardy in chocolate powder, a special Vardy's Volley ale was brewed and blue iced buns were on offer. People across the city donned blue for the day. Landmark buildings were lit up in blue, the street lights had blue bulbs and statues were decorated with City scarves.

The Premier League trophy was also brought to the town to be paraded in offices and public buildings so City fans could see the prize that was so tantalisingly close. Security guards stopped anyone from actually touching it, but in any case, informed football fans know you don't touch a trophy before it has been won. It is considered bad luck to do so. Another example of the superstitious nature of football fans.

The global media attention had also increased to almost epidemic proportions. People walking around the city were constantly being asked to stop to give their views – there were film crews on every street corner trying to capture the atmosphere around the city as its beloved football club was so close to making history. The city has a population of 330,000 and it felt like every one of them had been interviewed at some point.

Claudio Ranieri's pre-match press conference ahead of the Manchester United game was standing room only. The media suite at the King Power Stadium had seen some unbelievable scenes and plenty of comical moments during Ranieri's colourful press conferences, and there was still a hint of a garlic smell in the air from the Ranieri sausage a few weeks before, which Ranieri told the butchers to 'feed to my sharks', pointing to the journalists in front. The reporters would later be downgraded from sharks to piranhas.

The last time Ranieri had not shaken everyone's hand in the room because of the sheer number was ahead of the controversial draw with West Ham. He had returned to his pre-conference routine before the emphatic win over Swansea. Now he was faced with even more hands to shake. Was he superstitious too? He looked around the room. 'I have to shake everyone's hand,' he said as he set off on a marathon of handshakes.

As a fan it is ridiculous to think that what you may do on a match day could somehow affect events on the pitch, but that doesn't stop supporters from donning their lucky pants or shirt, visiting the same café or pub before the game, walking to the stadium by the same route and sitting in the same seat. They fear that one deviation from their routine could somehow impact on their team. Irrational it may be, but football fans don't take any risks. They don't wish to anger the football gods or tempt fate. There were lucky pants aplenty as City fans set off to Manchester on the morning of the game.

Old Trafford had been the scene of many title deciders, but usually it was United who were in contention themselves. Not this season. It had been a disappointing campaign for the United fans, despite reaching the FA Cup final. They were used to challenging for the biggest prize in domestic football. Their frustration must have been exacerbated by the fact that all their usual title rivals had also been off-colour and that it was a modest club like Leicester City who had taken advantage. It must have felt like an opportunity missed.

Arsenal, Chelsea and Manchester City must have been having similar thoughts. As a result, Manchester City and Chelsea had already announced managerial changes, while there were protests from Arsenal fans for a change at the Emirates. Van Gaal had also found himself the subject of speculation, with José Mourinho said to be waiting in the wings. That was a situation that Ranieri knew all about from his last season at Chelsea in 2004, when he had realised very quickly he was on borrowed time. Were Van Gaal's days numbered now? It was another subplot to an already intriguing and significant fixture.

United had been champions of England 20 times. City were going for their first ever title and Ranieri described it as a once-in-a-lifetime opportunity.

'Once in the life this could happen,' he said, 'that is football … once every 50 years a little team with less money can beat the biggest. Once. Everyone is behind us. There is a good feeling about this story. It is a good story but it is important to finish the story like an American movie, with a happy ending.'

The Blue Army were out in force and film crews gathered to record them as over 3,000 were making their way north. They were full of anticipation. City were one win away from pulling off the greatest sporting shock in history and there was a sense it could be a momentous, historic day at the Theatre of Dreams. What a fitting venue it would be to achieve the impossible dream.

The surroundings would be significant for a number of the players too. Danny Drinkwater had always dreamed of playing for United at Old Trafford and after coming through the academy with future City teammate Matty James (who was injured on this occasion) he came tantalisingly close but it never happened. Danny Simpson had made it into the Manchester United first team but only made three appearances before he was farmed out on loan to Royal Antwerp, Sunderland, Ipswich Town, Blackburn Rovers and finally Newcastle United. Eventually he realised his United dream would not come true and joined the Magpies permanently, before moving to Queens Park Rangers and ultimately Leicester.

Goalkeeper Kasper Schmeichel had never before played at the ground where his father had lifted so many Premier League titles. In the build-up to the game, some video footage emerged of a young Schmeichel playing football in the corridor near the dressing-rooms. He couldn't have been much older than seven or eight. And surprise, surprise, he was the keeper saving from Tom Ince, toddler son of his dad's then-teammate Paul Ince. Tom would go on to forge his own career too. The footage included a shot of Schmeichel getting hit in the face with the ball before crumpling to the ground in pain.

Twenty years on and Schmeichel was again diving around at Old Trafford, but now it was to stifle the United tide that threatened to wash City away in the opening 30 minutes. United struck first, through Anthony Martial, but Schmeichel was determined not to be beaten again, producing a string of fine saves. Then Wes Morgan grabbed an equaliser from a set-piece and the City fans were delirious. City had weathered the storm and actually looked the more likely to score the winner until Danny Drinkwater was shown a red card for two bookable offences. City were again grateful for Schmeichel in the closing stages as they held on. The players seemed dejected as the trudged off the pitch, as if it was an opportunity spurned.

City had come a long way to be disappointed with a draw at Old Trafford, but the fans weren't dejected. They celebrated for a good 20 minutes inside the ground again and when they eventually left an empty stadium, they carried on for another 30 minutes outside. They knew it could be a precious point. They knew it would apply that little bit more pressure to Tottenham when they travelled to Stamford Bridge to face Chelsea. There could be no margin for error. Spurs had to win at Chelsea for the first time in over 26 years if they were to keep the title race alive.

Monday 2 May 2016. The pubs and clubs across the county were packed to the rafters, while the vast majority of the populace of Leicestershire had tuned in from their homes to see if Chelsea would be true to their word and produce the performance against Tottenham Hotspur at Stamford Bridge that would see City crowned champions.

City's point at Old Trafford had meant that Spurs had to win. The pressure was on Mauricio Pochettino's side, and Chelsea – the outgoing champions – were determined that their crown would not be claimed by their city rivals. Eden Hazard and Cesc Fàbregas, who had both struggled to find their form during Chelsea's defence of the title (the worst in Premier League history, as it turned out), had both pledged that Chelsea were determined to do it for Leicester, as the rest of the world watched on in anticipation.

Well, not everyone. Claudio Ranieri had announced after the United game the day before that he was flying back to

Rome to take his 96-year-old mother out for lunch and would be airborne flying back home while the game was on.

The City players gathered around Jamie Vardy's house to watch the game: together, as they had been all season – although a couple of players weren't there. Marc Albrighton had sat and watched Spurs' thumping win over Stoke City two weeks before but had decided to take his fiancée out for dinner the following Monday when Spurs dropped two precious points against West Bromwich Albion, a result that put City on the brink of the title. As a result, he decided to repeat the trick in the hope that it would have some bearing on the outcome.

At half-time Albrighton's precautions appeared not to be having the desired effect. Goals from Harry Kane and Heung-min Son had put Spurs in control. City fans began to pencil in the visit of Everton the following Saturday as the date for destiny. But then something amazing happened. Spurs buckled. Gary Cahill raised the interest by pulling a goal back and the nerves started to show in the Spurs ranks as the game became increasingly fractious. There had been scuffles and incidents in the first half and it had looked as though Spurs may have been too pumped up for the game; then there were some terrible tackles in the second half and Spurs picked up nine yellow cards. It was amazing that there were still 22 players on the pitch.

Then, in the 83rd minute, Hazard fulfilled his promise to the City fans. He produced a wonderful, curling finish from the edge of the box which left Hugo Lloris, the Spurs goalkeeper, clutching at thin air. Anyone walking the streets of Leicester at that moment would have heard the communal roar of thousands of Foxes fans as the fairy-tale ending inched ever closer.

The numerous camera crews that had squeezed themselves into the pubs and clubs waited for the final whistle to capture the reaction as history was made. They weren't disappointed. As referee Mark Clattenburg blew the whistle the city erupted. Fans poured out of the pubs and from their homes to celebrate before heading en masse down to the King Power Stadium. Those who tried to drive to the stadium to witness the historic scenes found the streets clogged with cars blaring their horns, with passengers waving flags, all trying to make the same journey. Thousands partied until the early hours of the morning, while over at Vardy's house, where hundreds of fans and the waiting media had gathered outside, the party truly started. In fact, Vardy would later admit that some overzealous celebrating by certain large central defenders had left him with a repair bill for his television.

LEICESTER MERCURY BLOG, 3 MAY 2016
PREMIER LEAGUE CHAMPIONS

As Leicester City fans awoke with throbbing heads but joyous hearts this morning, they must have been asking themselves one question – was that all just a dream?

Even as they rubbed their bleary eyes and turned on the television to endless news reports about how City, the club that had been bottom of the Premier League for over 140 days of the previous season and were 5000-1 with some bookmakers to become English champions, had defied the odds to claim the Premier League crown, they must have thought they were either still asleep or in some bizarre parallel universe.

When they turned around and saw the empty champagne bottle on the kitchen side, flashbacks of the huge party the night before, sparked by Eden Hazard's amazing late equaliser against Tottenham Hotspur at Stamford Bridge, may have followed, but it would still seem too surreal to be true.

But it is. It is all true. Leicester City are Premier League champions. Even now, as you read these words, you are probably shaking your hungover heads in wonderment. You and the rest of the world.

How has a team of players who have all been rejected or passed over by other clubs been able to come together to defy the odds and pull off the greatest sporting shock in history?

How has a manager who was sacked after just four games as manager of Greece, having lost to the Faroe Islands, been able to pull together the same set of players who had faced what seemed to be certain relegation the season before and turned them into champions?

How has a club that has won just three League Cups in its 132-year history been able to break the dominance of English football's elite, to claim the ultimate prize in domestic football and become only the sixth team to lift the Premier League trophy?

It is an astonishing achievement which has left everyone scratching their heads in bewilderment and clapping their hands in admiration at the same time.

The scenes outside the King Power Stadium last night and throughout today were amazing. City fans descended on their Mecca to worship their club and celebrate what many would admit was the greatest moment of their lives. The party is set to continue for quite some time as well.

People from all walks of life, from different faiths and cultural backgrounds have all been brought together by one amazing achievement. Football unites communities and brings civic pride like nothing else. Leicester people are always proud to say they are from Leicester, but even more so now.

The people of Leicester have puffed-up chests and heads held high because their football team has put the city on the map, quite literally in terms of the rest of the world who didn't even seem to know where Leicester was until this season.

They soon found it. The world's media has camped out for weeks in the city waiting for the moment when the fairy-tale would come true. The Leicester City story has captured the imagination of people the world over because it is the greatest rags-to-riches underdog story in sporting history.

Less than 15 years ago City was a club on its knees. The very future of the club was in doubt. The thought of challenging for a Premier League title in future years seemed ridiculous. There was the danger of there not being a future.

Then there was relegation to League One for the first time in the club's history in 2008, another dark time for the City fans. It is fair to say there have been more downs than ups.

That is why the rest of the football community will not begrudge City this incredible moment. City fans, who wear their shirts with pride, have been applauded as they walk down the street. The travelling fans and Ranieri's incredible team have been given standing ovations by rival fans at various grounds around the country, including at Old Trafford last Sunday.

Football supporters have cast aside the usual tribalism because they recognise that what City have achieved is extraordinary. It can potentially change the landscape of the Premier League. The elite clubs must now reflect on their approach and raise their game, while the clubs of City's ilk now have belief that they can aspire to follow City's lead. They can dream as well.

When the Thai owners came to the club in 2010 there was some scepticism. Previous foreign ownerships at English clubs had gone spectacularly wrong. They had been disasters. City fans may have thought, with their luck, this would be another one. The Srivaddhanaprabha family have been astonishing. Not only have they committed their substantial wealth, writing off £103 million of loans into equity, they have not abused their ownership, cherishing the history and traditions of the club. They may not come from an English football culture but they have shown great respect to the supporters. The club is the fans' cherished baby and they have demonstrated it is in safe hands.

Even when their judgement was being questioned last summer when they replaced Nigel Pearson, who deserves an immense amount of credit for getting the club turned around and the ball rolling again during his two spells in charge, with Ranieri they have been proven right. They are shrewd operators.

As for Ranieri, finally the bridesmaid has become the bride and on Saturday, when the Premier League trophy is presented to City captain Wes Morgan after the last home game of the season he will have his big day.

Four times he has been in a title race and four times he has finished second, in Italy, France and England. Finally, Ranieri, the man who has entertained everyone this season with his genial, lovable antics, colourful turn of phrase and warmth, is a champion. The man from Rome has conquered Leicester, just as his ancestors did so many centuries ago.

After the departure of Esteban Cambiasso, City's player of the year last season, Ranieri sat before the media and tried to raise spirits. 'Cambiasso is a great champion and now we have to find another great champion,' he said. He had 24 of them right under his Roman nose.

To a man they have been magnificent. From Kasper Schmeichel in goal to Jamie Vardy scoring 22 goals and leading the attack; from the skipper Wes Morgan to the longest-serving player Andy King, who has been with City through their League One, Championship and now Premier League title triumphs; from the mercurial winger Riyad Mahrez, the greatest £400,000 signing in the modern game, to the voracious predator that is N'Golo Kanté. Every single one of them has played a huge part.

They have all shown a burning desire, a hunger that has been the driving force behind their success. They have all faced disappointment and rejection in their lives but have had the character to keep going. That is why they didn't buckle during the season when pundits were predicting they would. Those dark moments provided an inner strength that has proved so crucial. They were character-building. While their rivals seemed to wilt under pressure, City were able to stay strong.

Around the stadium there are now poster pictures of each player hanging from the lamp posts, but the memory of what these players have achieved will live on long after those flags are pulled down. As Gary Lineker, City's favourite son, has said, they will now be immortals.

Finally, the supporters. The Blue Army. They have played their role. When City have been behind in games they have roared even more. When the players have needed their help, they have been there. They have travelled the length and breadth of the country and left their mark. The sight of them remaining in the away ends of empty grounds, singing their songs, long after their rivals have gone, refusing to move, will live long in the memory.

The secret to Leicester City's success is easy. It has just been one glorious team effort by everyone.

City were the champions of England, but it still didn't feel real. The next morning the first question City fans asked themselves was 'Did that really happen?'. But there were plenty of reminders lying around Leicester to confirm it had, as bottles and cans littered the streets around the stadium. But that wasn't the end of the celebrations; it was just the beginning. Cars continued to beep as they drove by and fans were still making their way down to the stadium throughout the day. Word spread that the City players and Ranieri had been taken out for a celebratory lunch after training, which went ahead as usual despite the late night (some of the players had carried on celebrating in a local nightclub). Hundreds of fans blocked the street outside the restaurant and police eventually had to escort the players away. En route to the restaurant, Vardy spotted a Vardy double, complete with full City kit and sporting his trademark wrist support. He ordered the bus driver to stop and called for his double to join the party, which he did.

Later, Ranieri arrived at the training ground to meet a group of waiting reporters, who gave him a rousing reception as he entered the room. Having come so close on so many occasions, Ranieri had finally won a title.

'It was an amazing achievement,' he said. 'It was unbelievable. We wanted to do something special but nobody could think about what we have achieved now. It is an amazing season for us. I am very, very pleased. In my mind always I believe I have to win a title. I want to win – now I have … This is, for me, my strength: always I am a positive man, always I believed that I could achieve something.'

Captain Wes Morgan, who had only been playing in the Premier League for two seasons, couldn't believe it. 'It's the best feeling of my career and I couldn't be prouder that it's as part of this team,' he said. 'Everyone's worked so hard for this, nobody believed we could do it, but here we are, Premier League champions and deservedly so. I've never known a spirit like the one between these boys, we're like brothers. People saw it last season when everyone expected us to be relegated, but we fought back to prove people wrong. Saturday can't come quickly enough. I can't wait to get my hands on the trophy.'

Even the news that his central defensive partner Robert Huth had been banned for three games for clashing with Marouane Fellaini, forcing him out of the Everton game which would now be the biggest party Leicester had ever seen, didn't dampen the mood. Huth vowed to go 'full John Terry', teasing his former Chelsea teammate, who had celebrated in full kit when Chelsea won the Champions League, despite missing the match through suspension. He was true to his word.

In a rare interview, Leicester City vice-chairman Aiyawatt Srivaddhanaprabha vowed that this was just the start. He said they were looking at either increasing the size of the King Power Stadium or even moving to a new, bigger stadium, while he also revealed talks would take place over new contracts for the players and Ranieri, to reward them for their efforts and ward off suitors. He also vowed to make vital funds available to strengthen the squad, as the title had also guaranteed that not only would City be competing in the Champions League, they would be seeded for the group stages.

'I didn't just say we would win the league, but I said we would do everything we can to bring the club success,' he said. 'Yeah, my father stated in 2013, when we got promoted, that we would try and fight in the next three to four years for the Champions League. Now we are in the Champions League he got what he wanted, but it was another bonus that we won the league!'

As for the controversial decision to appoint Ranieri, Aiywatt, known as Top, had been totally vindicated. 'At that time there were a number of managers I got in to interview,' he said. 'Claudio was my first choice – even though I had three or four more to interview. He had something special on that day and in his interview when he spoke he said everything that was in my head. I don't know how he did that! He said everything I wanted to hear. All the plans I had in my head, he said them out loud. The character you can see, he was the one that could move the club forward for sure.'

While Top was keen to direct the praise on to Ranieri, his staff and players, the Srivaddhanaprabha family had undoubtedly played a huge role. City's transformation simply would not have been possible without their investment and guidance. They had paid £39 million for the club and £17 million to buy the stadium, and had written off £103 million worth of loans by converting them into equity. Now they were set to get their return on their investment – not a monetary return; rather the respect and admiration of thousands of Foxes fans. Their reputation back in Thailand and around the world had also been enhanced. Thai-owned Leicester City were kings of the Premier League, the most high-profile league in the world.

LEICESTER MERCURY BLOG, 4 MAY 2016
THE CITY CELEBRATES

If you live or work in Leicester the last few days will live long in the memory.

Regardless of whether you are a football fan or a Leicester City supporter, you will never forget where you were and what you were doing when Leicester became Premier League champions, or the celebrations since.

Some of the memories of the huge street party following the moment City won the title on Monday night may be a little hazy, but you will never forget the emotion and pride that everyone across the city and county has felt since Claudio Ranieri's men were confirmed as Premier League champions.

I had a feeling the ensuing days would feel surreal on Saturday when something very strange happened. I was walking my dog over the fields near to my house when I saw a fox spring out of the bushes in front of me and skulk, keeping a careful eye on me and my Springer Spaniel, Molly, across the field. It was 2pm and there was brilliant sunshine.

I have seen plenty of foxes but never in broad daylight. I thought: how confident, how bold, how brave, how #fearless. I took it as a sign.

The next day I headed down to the King Power Stadium early. It was the morning of the Manchester United game, the day City could clinch the title on their own terms with a win at Old Trafford, the Theatre of Dreams. It felt like fate that City should win the title at such a cathedral of English football, a ground that had seen so many titles sealed on its turf.

I watched as fans began to gather to jump on the 25 coaches that were heading up to Manchester. There was a sense of expectation, that this could be the day when the unbelievable became reality, when their dreams could come true.

At Old Trafford I was asked to do a pitch-side interview for a television crew and as I stood next to the touchline, I stared at the spot where Sir Alex Ferguson and Brian Kidd had jumped onto the pitch in celebration when United won their first Premier League title in 1993. I wondered if we would soon be seeing Claudio Ranieri and Craig Shakespeare sliding to their knees and kissing the turf in similar fashion a few hours later.

City's performance that day epitomised what Ranieri's men had been about all season. They had to stay strong as United put them under immense pressure for the first 30 minutes. Even after Anthony Martial opened the scoring, City never wilted. Wes Morgan scored the equaliser and skidded on his knees, Kidd-style, in front of the ecstatic 3,000 travelling City fans.

The game could have gone either way, but at the end it was a fair result. The players looked a little crestfallen as they left the field, sensing it was an opportunity missed to put the title to bed, but the City fans were ecstatic. Once again they refused to leave the stadium, chanting their repertoire, and when they did eventually vacate the away end, the party continued just outside the stadium for another half an hour.

It was a point closer to the title, it was one hand on the trophy. That point put a huge psychological weight on Tottenham Hotspur, who now had to beat Chelsea the very next night at Stamford Bridge for the first time in 26 years to keep the title race alive.

Individually, the fact that so many of City's players have experienced difficult times during their careers had given them a mental strength to hold on at United. Mentally, it seemed Spurs crumbled at Stamford Bridge, throwing away a two-goal lead as their discipline completely deserted them.

Pubs and clubs across Leicester were packed with supporters who wanted to share with each other what could be a historic moment, while fans from across the globe sent the *Mercury* pictures of themselves watching the game in homes and bars in far-flung places.

With Spurs 2-0 up at half-time, thoughts were turning to Saturday's visit of Everton as the next possible date with destiny, but then Gary Cahill pulled a goal back. Suddenly, it had got really interesting. Another Chelsea goal and City would be on the verge of greatness.

You could sense Spurs were tightening up, growing anxious. You could feel that an equaliser was coming. Eden Hazard had been missing for Chelsea all season, but he had declared, along with Cesc Fàbregas, his desire for City to become champions ahead of Spurs, and he came out of hiding.

I remember when Michael Thomas scored Arsenal's second and title-clinching goal in a thrilling decider at Liverpool in 1989 and recalled the words of commentator Brian Moore – 'It's up for grabs now' – as Hazard curled in that wonderful equaliser.

City fans waited with bated breath for the final whistle but Spurs looked down and out. The title race was over the moment Hazard produced the one piece of magic he had conjured all season.

Leicester exploded into rapture when referee Mark Clattenburg blew the final whistle. Car horns were blaring, flags were waving and City fans were singing 'Champione' as they all congregated towards their place of worship, the King Power Stadium, for an incredible street party that was still going on well into the following night.

The next morning I had a Mr Benn moment. Mr Benn was a children's television character who would go off to a fancy-dress shop and put on a costume that would transport him to have an adventure somewhere, and on his return there would always been a keepsake to remind him that what had happened had been real. The next morning I walked, bleary eyed, into my kitchen and there on the side was a champagne cork. It had happened. I hadn't dreamt it.

I was back down the King Power Stadium by 7am and there was a group of City staff clearing up the debris from the party the night before while cars were still driving past, beeping at the massed ranks of media now gathering to tell the incredible story of City's title triumph.

Later that day I headed down to the training ground, along with a collection of journalists, to meet the triumphant Ranieri.

We had to wait a while. Ranieri and the players had been taken to San Carlo restaurant in Granby Street by the owners for a celebratory lunch. Word had got out and hundreds of supporters gathered outside to cheer their heroes. The players couldn't leave for the crowd and had to be rescued by police.

Eventually, Ranieri walked into the room to a standing ovation from the journalists. Many members of the media had expressed their view that Ranieri had been the wrong man for the job, a bad fit for City, and had expected him to be one of the first Premier League managers to be shown the door. They had been sharpening the quills to write his epitaph as City boss.

Now they were showing their admiration for Ranieri and City's incredible accomplishment. Some managers might have taken this as an opportunity to gloat, to throw it back into the faces of the doubters. Not Ranieri. He has conducted himself with such dignity all season, he was better than that.

After 30 minutes he finished, stood up and said to the writers: 'This is why I love English football because there is respect. I know if we don't do so well you will criticise me but I respect you and you respect me.' How could you have anything but respect for a gentleman like Ranieri?

Then it was back down the stadium for more interviews and I found the party was getting back into full swing again.

The De Montfort gospel choir were conducting a sing-along with City fans while cars continued to crawl down the congested Raw Dykes Road, still beeping their horns and waving their flags.

As I waited to be interviewed by Channel 4, a fire engine came past. The siren came on and members of the fire crew started punching the air and celebrating with the City fans, who raced into the road to join them.

During the interview, I was asked about the cultural diversity of the city and whether it was reflected in the support for the football club. I told the presenter to just look behind us because there stood a collection of people who typified the diversity of the city. There were people from all races, creeds and colours standing side-by-side, united in their support for a football team, a team that is also as diverse as the community they represent.

The team have played as one this season. As people ponder how this miracle has been possible, they need only look at the unity and spirit within the ranks of the squad for the main reason.

Football brings a community together like nothing else. Leicester City unite the people.

The Premier League trophy would be presented at the King Power Stadium after the Everton match. Typically, the owners wanted to share the big day with the fans, putting on events and handing out free drinks and pizza, while Andrea Bocelli, who had contacted his fellow countryman Claudio Ranieri to ask if he could sing at City's celebrations, serenaded the champions before the game.

After all the pomp, ceremony and celebrations there was

actually a football match to be played and City didn't want to spoil the party by being below par, as they had two years ago when they were beaten 4-1 by Brighton, days after clinching promotion to the Premier League. There was no fear of that. City looked every inch the champions. Everton, who must have felt like unwanted gatecrashers, were simply no match for Ranieri's men. Andy King picked out Jamie Vardy for City's first before King, who had been with City every step of the way from League One to the Premier League title, suitably scored the second after more sublime skill from Riyad Mahrez. The visitors briefly threatened to make a game of it at the start of the second half but when Matthew Pennington tripped Vardy in the area and the City striker smashed home his 24th goal of an astonishing season from the penalty spot, the game was all but done.

Vardy was chasing Tottenham's Harry Kane for the Premier League Golden Boot, and he had a great opportunity to complete his hat-trick and draw level with Kane when Mahrez put him through, but Joel Robles denied him with his legs. Then Darron Gibson tripped Schlupp inside the area and Vardy had a second penalty. Unfortunately, with adrenalin buzzing, he smashed his spot-kick over the bar and high into the Kop. 'I think it was heading for that helicopter which was flying overhead,' joked Vardy afterwards. He would later learn that he was the football writers' player of the year.

There were muted cheers from the away end when Kevin Mirallas pulled a goal back but Everton were just playing a supporting role to the main event.

After the game, the atmosphere of anticipation continued to grow as the stages were set. Fittingly, Alan Birchenall, the club ambassador who had served the club for 40 years in various capacities and had witnessed all the low points, was now asked to carry out the trophy that marked the club's greatest-ever triumph.

As the trophy was presented – by a fan who had won a competition – captain Morgan looked down at the ground and then back to the trophy, as if he was just checking it was all real. He and Ranieri raised the trophy high above their heads and the celebrations began again.

After a lap of honour with all the staff, owners and their families, Ranieri came into the post-match press conference, which was then invaded by Kasper Schmeichel, holding the trophy, and Christian Fuchs, the latter emptying the best part of a full bottle of champagne over Ranieri's head in front of the watching media.

Ranieri had laid the foundations for sides that had won titles before, leaving others to reap the rewards after he had left. Now the role was reversed. Ranieri had taken Nigel Pearson's solid foundations and built something incredible on them. He said he would keep his medal close and use it when those difficult times came again.

'I will keep it in my home and when there is a bad moment I will take it out, look at it and say, "Heh, come on man, balance",' he said. 'I think it was an amazing moment for me because I'm not the youngest and there is another test now. You are the champion of the Premier League and it's something special for everybody. I've lost the finals in England, Spain and Italy but for me to win this is something special.'

The celebrations continued into the club's end-of-season awards dinner, where Riyad Mahrez was named player of the year and N'Golo Kanté was players' player of the year; Vardy won goal of the season for his strike against Liverpool, while Jeff Schlupp was given the young player of the year accolade.

Vardy would also pick up the Football Writers' Association player of the year award and was named as the

Premier League player of the year, although he was quick to point out that the honour had to be shared with his teammates. 'We've just won the league,' he said, almost having to remind himself of the enormity of what they had achieved. 'It's unbelievable. I don't think words can describe it, to be honest with you. You've just seen with the celebrations with all the fans and players; it's unimaginable. It's frightening. It's unbelievable the team spirit we've got. It's astounding how we are together. We are like brothers.'

But there was still one game to go. Ranieri was to return to Stamford Bridge for the first time since he was given a guard of honour by his players as he left his position, having been sacked by Roman Abramovich in 2004. Now he was returning and again he was to be given a guard of honour. Only this time it was because he was returning as a Premier League champion.

'It's amazing,' said Ranieri in the build-up to the final game. 'I've been there [Stamford Bridge] with Juventus in the Champions League but this time is different because I'm manager of Leicester – another English club. It's emotional. I hope my old fans are happy with me.

'When I came here I saw the last match was at Chelsea. Now, I come back as a champion. Unbelievable. A good story! Let me live this, with emotion. Of course it is something different now. I want to thank them. I watched some of them hold up placards with "do it for Ranieri" on Monday [against Tottenham]. It was amazing. I want to thank them.

'My players gave me a guard of honour. Marcel Desailly and John Terry called all their teammates together because they knew my job had finished there. I think it was one of the more important moments of my sporting life. They did it on the pitch. One man, Gary Staker [a member of Chelsea's backroom staff], who is an amazing man, called me to the centre of the pitch and the players made the guard of honour so when I turned around I saw; it was amazing.'

When Claudio Ranieri did step out of the darkness of the Stamford Bridge tunnel on 15 May 2016 and into the bright sunlight, he was greeted by a standing ovation from all corners of the ground. You don't win trophies for being popular but the former Chelsea and now all-conquering City boss is evidence, if any was needed, that nice guys can win.

The press called him the Tinkerman, the City fans call him the Godfather, the players call him gaffer, the Leicestershire MPs want him called Sir Claudio, but whatever guise he goes by, Ranieri will always be remembered as the man who created history, whose achievements with City have changed perceptions of what is possible in the Premier League.

It was fitting that City arrived at Stamford Bridge on the last stop of what had been an incredible campaign, not just because Ranieri had his fairy-tale ending with Abramovich, the man who didn't believe in him, looking on from his executive box. (The pair briefly met before the game, down the tunnel, and it was a warm encounter.) This was also the ground where City's Premier League adventure really began, on 23 August 2014. City had returned to the Premier League after a decade in the Championship and League One. It was their first away game of the campaign. Everything was new, fresh and exciting and while City played well that day they were ultimately outclassed by a side that would go on to win the title that season.

That game had demonstrated how much learning they had to do, how much this group of players had to grow. Kasper Schmeichel, Wes Morgan, Andy King, Jeff Schlupp, Riyad Mahrez and Leonardo Ulloa had all started the game that day. Marcin Wasilewski and Marc Albrighton were on the substitutes' bench. All of them were now returning having made that incredible journey from being Premier League rookies to champions of England.

It was also on the Stamford Bridge turf that the title was finally won, when Eden Hazard scored the goal that ended Spurs' title hopes. When the line-ups were announced before the match, the Foxes fans cheered Hazard's name as loudly as those of the City players, and broke into a chorus of 'Eden Hazard is a Blue'.

The game ended in a 1-1 draw. Danny Drinkwater scored a superb equaliser for City in the 82nd minute to cancel out Cesc Fàbregas's second-half penalty following Jeff Schlupp's trip on Nemanja Matić. The result meant City finished with a ten-point lead over Arsenal, who overtook Spurs to clinch second when Spurs collapsed at relegated Newcastle United. Ten points. Those who still sneered at City and said they had been lucky with injuries or penalty decisions couldn't deny that to win a league by such a distance was incredible for any club, but for a team that was bottom of the table for 140 days of the previous season it was quite extraordinary.

Both sets of fans sang Ranieri's name throughout an entertaining game, played in a sporting atmosphere, and at the final whistle he went across to the away end with his players to applaud them for their outstanding support during the season. Then, with his name ringing around the stadium, he slowly and quietly walked away on his own, back down that tunnel. It was the walk of a man who had proved a point, a man who had answered his critics. It was the walk of a champion.

After the game defender Danny Simpson admitted it had all been difficult to believe, that this group of players, this band of brothers, had become champions of England.

'It has been an unbelievable journey this season and I don't want it to stop,' said Simpson. 'We have only lost three games all season and that takes some doing in the Premier League. I have enjoyed every single minute of it. It still hasn't sunk in yet. It might sink in now over the next couple of weeks now we have no more games to play.

'I still look at that medal and can't believe it. I have hidden the medal but I keep getting it out to see it and put it around my neck. Friends and family keep coming around to see it as well. It is a special medal. To win the league by ten points says it all. It is some going. It isn't a Leicester team that has scraped the league by a few points, we have won it by ten points. That is credit to everyone, the players and staff, and the manager, everyone who has been involved.'

17 MAY 2016
VICTORY PARADE

Leicester City's Premier League party is in full swing. Well, it has been for some time.

It is hard enough to believe that Leicester City, the club I have covered for the past seven seasons, ever since they gained promotion back to the Championship from the third tier of English football, are now champions of England.

It was astonishing to see nearly 250,000 people line the streets of Leicester to catch a glimpse of the open-top bus parade with Claudio Ranieri and his players lapping up every second, before arriving at Victoria Park where 70,000 had gathered.

A sea of blue flags waved as each player was introduced to the crowd before captain Wes Morgan, Ranieri and owner

Vichai Srivaddhanaprabha held the trophy aloft again as fireworks illuminated the twilight. The party wasn't over as Leicester rock band Kasabian came out to play a free set for their fellow Foxes fans, including City anthems 'Fire', which is played after every City goal at the King Power Stadium, and the aptly titled 'Underdog'.

The party went on into the night as the masses walked back down London Road to continue the celebrations. It was simply surreal.

I look at the final league table and it seems even more incredible. City haven't just won the title, they have walked it. Ten points was the final gap between City and second-placed Arsenal. And yet, even earlier this week, I heard some people in the media, who had probably predicted City's demise throughout the campaign, stating that City have been lucky, that their title is more to do with the failings of others than City's quality. I even heard one reporter state he was putting money on them to be relegated next season. They still can't shed their underdog tag.

It is hard to imagine they can repeat this success, but then again it was hard to imagine this was possible in the first place. However, to win the league by ten points is down to so much more than luck.

It is down to good leadership and wise investment from the owners, good management from the board, brilliant leadership from Claudio Ranieri, an immaculate attention to detail from all his staff, and the work ethic, camaraderie and team spirit of the players. Plus a sprinkling of magic dust.

Yes, it is hard to comprehend how a team that was bottom of the table for so long the previous campaign can end the season standing on a stage in Victoria Park, raising the Premier League trophy aloft in front of a sea of waving blue and white flags, but this is no fluke. In their last 47 league games they have lost just four times. Only Chelsea, Arsenal (twice) and Liverpool have managed to get the better of them. Incredible.

Ranieri would savour his greatest-ever achievement and soak up the adulation, but already he was thinking of what was next for Leicester City.

'We have achieved something amazing, unbelievable,' he said. 'We know it won't be a fairy tale next season, but it won't be a nightmare. It will be different next season but of course we are fighting. All the big teams will be back to the top, but we will continue to fight. That is our destiny. It was important to be ready when the other big teams were not.

'The Champions League will be a very good experience for my players. It will be a very good atmosphere with the music and I hope we are ready – not just to listen to the music but to make some music.'

Despite their seeding as champions of England, Leicester City will start their Champions League campaign as the underdogs, the rank outsiders. The bookmakers have priced them at 100-1 to become champions of Europe. Would you bet against them?

MAY SUMMARY

Competition	Date	Fixture
Premier League	Sun 1 May	Man Utd 1-1 Leicester
Premier League	Mon 2 May	Chelsea 2-2 Tottenham*
* LEICESTER CITY ARE CHAMPIONS		
Premier League	Sat 7 May	Leicester 3-1 Everton
Premier League	Sun 15 May	Chelsea 1-1 Leicester

*On Monday 2 May 2016, 5000-1 shots Leicester City
are confirmed as Premier League champions*

FINAL LEAGUE STANDINGS

		P	W	D	L	GF	GA	GD	Pts
1	Leicester City	38	23	12	3	68	36	32	81
2	Arsenal	38	20	11	7	65	36	29	71
3	Tottenham Hotspur	38	19	13	6	69	35	34	70
4	Manchester City	38	19	9	10	71	41	30	66

End of Season

APPENDICES

APPENDIX 1

LEICESTER CITY RESULTS 2015/16

Competition	Date	Fixture
AUGUST 2015		
Premier League	Sat 8 Aug	Leicester 4-2 Sunderland
Premier League	Sat 15 Aug	West Ham 1-2 Leicester
Premier League	Sat 22 Aug	Leicester 1-1 Tottenham
League Cup – Second Round	Tue 25 Aug	Bury 1-4 Leicester
Premier League	Sat 29 Aug	Bournemouth 1-1 Leicester
SEPTEMBER 2015		
Premier League	Sun 13 Sep	Leicester 3-2 Aston Villa
Premier League	Sat 19 Sep	Stoke 2-2 Leicester
League Cup – Third Round	Tue 22 Sep	Leicester 2-1 West Ham
Premier League	Sat 26 Sep	Leicester 2-5 Arsenal
OCTOBER 2015		
Premier League	Sat 3 Oct	Norwich 1-2 Leicester
Premier League	Sat 17 Oct	Southampton 2-2 Leicester
Premier League	Sat 24 Oct	Leicester 1-0 Crystal Palace
League Cup – Fourth Round	Tue 27 Oct	Hull 1-1 Leicester (Hull City win 5-4 on penalties)

Competition	Date	Fixture
	NOVEMBER 2015	
Competition	Date	Fixture
Premier League	Sat 7 Nov	Leicester 2-1 Watford
Premier League	Sat 21 Nov	Newcastle 0-3 Leicester
Premier League	Sat 28 Nov	Leicester 1-1 Man Utd
	DECEMBER 2015	
Premier League	Sat 5 Dec	Swansea 0-3 Leicester
Premier League	Mon 14 Dec	Leicester 2-1 Chelsea
Premier League	Sat 19 Dec	Everton 2-3 Leicester
Premier League	Sat 26 Dec	Liverpool 1-0 Leicester
Premier League	Tue 29 Dec	Leicester 0-0 Man City
	JANUARY 2016	
Premier League	Sat 2 Jan	Leicester 0-0 Bournemouth
FA Cup – Third Round	Sun 10 Jan	Tottenham 2-2 Leicester
Premier League	Wed 13 Jan	Tottenham 0-1 Leicester
Premier League	Sat 16 Jan	Aston Villa 1-1 Leicester
FA Cup – Third Round	Wed 20 Jan	Leicester 0-2 Tottenham
Premier League	Sat 23 Jan	Leicester 3-0 Stoke
	FEBRUARY 2016	
Premier League	Tue 2 Feb	Leicester 2-0 Liverpool
Premier League	Sat 6 Feb	Man City 1-3 Leicester
Premier League	Sun 14 Feb	Arsenal 2-1 Leicester
Premier League	Sat 27 Feb	Leicester 1-0 Norwich
	MARCH 2016	
Premier League	Tue 1 Mar	Leicester 2-2 West Brom
Premier League	Sat 5 Mar	Watford 0-1 Leicester
Premier League	Mon 14 Mar	Leicester 1-0 Newcastle
Premier League	Sat 19 Mar	Crystal Palace 0-1 Leicester

Competition	Date	Fixture
	APRIL 2016	
Premier League	Sun 3 Apr	Leicester 1-0 Southampton
Premier League	Sun 10 Apr	Sunderland 0-2 Leicester
Premier League	Sun 17 Apr	Leicester 2-2 West Ham
Premier League	Sun 24 Apr	Leicester 4-0 Swansea
	MAY 2016	
Premier League	Sun 1 May	Man Utd 1-1 Leicester
Premier League	Mon 1 May	Chelsea 2-2 Tottenham*
	* LEICESTER CITY ARE CHAMPIONS	
Premier League	Sat 7 May	Leicester 3-1 Everton
Premier League	Sun 15 May	Chelsea 1-1 Leicester

APPENDIX 2

HOW LEICESTER CITY'S TITLE ODDS CHANGED THROUGHOUT THE SEASON WITH WILLIAM HILL

5000-1 – pre-season

2500-1 – 5 September (international break after four matches; Leicester had beaten Sunderland and West Ham and drawn with Bournemouth and Tottenham

5000-1 – 3 October (after winning away at Norwich; elsewhere, a comfortable win for Manchester City over Newcastle saw Leicester drift in the betting as Manuel Pellegrini's team became 4-6 favourites)

1000-1 – 17 October (after drawing at Southampton)

750-1 – 24 October (after winning at home to Crystal Palace)

500-1 – 31 October (after winning at West Brom)

200-1 – 7 November (after winning at home to Watford)

100-1 – 22 November (the day after winning at Newcastle)

50-1 – 28 November (after drawing at home with Manchester United)

33-1 – 5 December (after winning at Swansea)

20-1 – 14 December (after winning at home to Chelsea)

12-1 – 27 December (the day after losing at Liverpool)

25-1 – 2 January (after drawing at home with Bournemouth, having also drawn with Man City on 29 December)

10-1 – 14 January (the day after winning at Tottenham)

8-1 – 24 January (after Arsenal lost at home to Chelsea,
and the day after Leicester beat Stoke at home and
Manchester City drew against West Ham)

9-2 – 2 February (after winning at home to Liverpool)

7-4 – 6 February (after winning at Manchester City) –
THE FIRST TIME LEICESTER ARE PRICED AS TITLE FAVOURITES

6-4 – 14 February (after losing at Arsenal; elsewhere,
Manchester City lost at home to Spurs)

Evens – 14 March (after winning at home to Newcastle;
Manchester City had drawn away at Norwich on the 12th,
while Spurs had won away at Aston Villa on the 13th)

8-15 – 19 March (after winning at Crystal Palace)

1-3 – 3 April (after winning at home to Southampton)

1-6 – 10 April (after winning at home to Sunderland;
elsewhere, Spurs won at home to Manchester United)

1-4 – 17 April (after drawing at home with West Ham)

4-9 – 18 April (after Spurs won away at Stoke)

1-6 – 24 April – (after winning at home to Swansea)

1-20 – 25 April (after Spurs drew at home to West Brom)

1-16 – 2 May (the day after drawing at Manchester
United; Spurs were to face Chelsea in the evening)

APPENDIX 3

LEICESTER CITY APPEARANCES 2015/16

	Player	Position	Total	League	Cup
11	Marc Albrighton	Midfielder	42	38	4
1	Kasper Schmeichel	Goalkeeper	40	38	2
14	N'Golo Kanté	Midfielder	40	37	3
26	Riyad Mahrez	Midfielder	39	37	2
20	Shinji Okazaki	Striker	39	36	3
5	Wes Morgan	Defender	38	38	0
9	Jamie Vardy	Striker	38	36	2
4	Danny Drinkwater	Midfielder	37	35	2
6	Robert Huth	Defender	35	35	0
28	Christian Fuchs	Defender	34	32	2
23	Leonardo Ulloa	Striker	33	29	4
17	Danny Simpson	Defender	32	30	2
10	Andy King	Midfielder	29	25	4
15	Jeff Schlupp	Midfielder	26	24	2
24	Nathan Dyer	Midfielder	14	12	2
22	Demarai Gray	Midfielder	14	12	2
33	Gökhan Inler	Midfielder	10	5	5
27	Marcin Wasilewski	Defender	9	4	5
13	Daniel Amartey	Midfielder	5	5	0
19	Andrej Kramarić	Striker	5	2	3
32	Mark Schwarzer	Goalkeeper	3	0	3
30	Ben Chilwell	Defender	3	0	3
18	Liam Moore	Defender	1	0	1
8	Matty James	Midfielder	0	0	0
12	Ben Hamer	Goalkeeper	0	0	0

APPENDIX 4

LEICESTER CITY GOALSCORERS 2015/16

Player	League	FA Cup	League Cup	Total
Jamie Vardy	24	0	0	24
Riyad Mahrez	17	0	1	18
Shinji Okazaki	5	1	0	6
Leonardo Ulloa	6	0	0	6
Joseph Dodoo	0	0	4	4
Robert Huth	3	0	0	3
Andy King	2	0	1	3
Marc Albrighton	2	0	0	2
Daniel Drinkwater	2	0	0	2
Nathan Dyer	1	0	1	2
Wes Morgan	2	0	0	2
N'Golo Kanté	1	0	0	1
Andrej Kramarić	0	0	1	1
Jeff Schlupp	1	0	0	1
Marcin Wasilewski	0	1	0	1

GEOFF HURST'S GREATS
ENGLAND'S 1966 HERO SELECTS HIS FINEST EVER FOOTBALLERS

England's 1966 World Cup hero brings exclusive
anecdotes and analysis as he ranks football's greats.

ISBN 978-178578-050-9 (paperback) / 978-178578-156-8 (ebook)

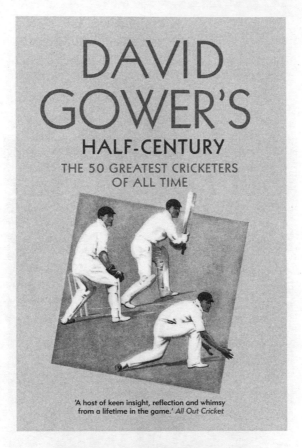

MESSI
MORE THAN A SUPERSTAR

Bestselling portrait of the greatest footballer
of our time – an unrivalled behind-the-scenes
look at the life of a football superstar.

ISBN 978-190685-091-3 (paperback) / 978-190685-092-0 (ebook)

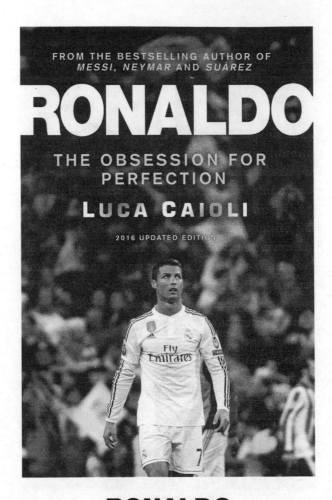

FROM THE BESTSELLING AUTHOR OF
MESSI, NEYMAR AND *SUÁREZ*

RONALDO

THE OBSESSION FOR PERFECTION

LUCA CAIOLI

2016 UPDATED EDITION

RONALDO
THE OBSESSION
FOR PERFECTION

The inside track on the global superstar; *Ronaldo* lays
bare the career of a modern footballing icon.

ISBN 978-190685-093-7 (paperback) / 978-190685-094-4 (ebook)

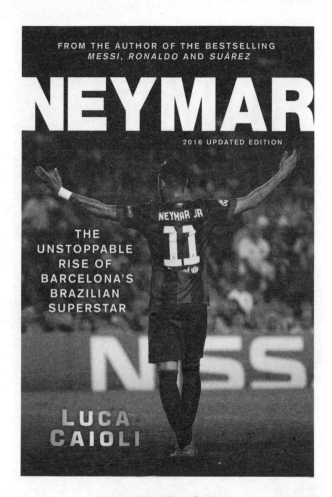

NEYMAR
THE UNSTOPPABLE RISE OF BARCELONA'S BRAZILIAN SUPERSTAR

A revealing portrait of one of the greats of the
modern game, featuring exclusive interviews with
those who have known and worked with him.

ISBN 978-190685-095-1 (paperback) / 978-190685-096-8 (ebook)

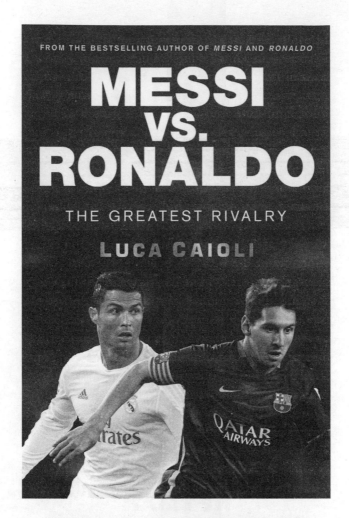

MESSI VS. RONALDO
THE GREATEST RIVALRY

The goals, the trophies, the lifestyles – Luca Caioli
tells the inside story of football's greatest rivalry.

ISBN 978-178578-055-4 (paperback) / 978-178578-056-1 (ebook)